The Possibility of Me

A Mémoire in Three Movements

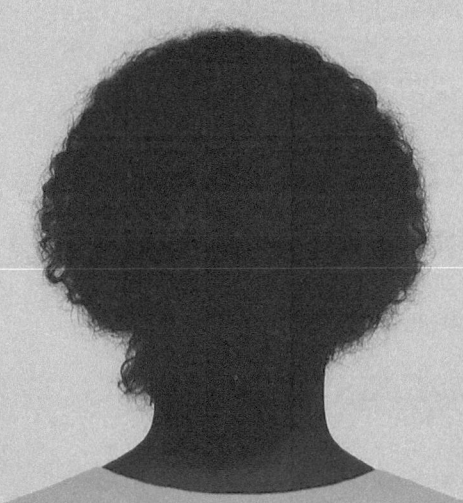

BRIANNA MILLER

Upcoming Titles by On Paper Press

You Are The Possibility
by Brianna Miller
Expected drop: July/August 2025

Letters to My Teachers: What I Wish My Teachers Knew
by Mikeila Miller
Expected drop: August 2025

White Supremacy Culture Revisited: The Traits That Survive Us
by Brianna Miller
Expected drop: August/September 2025

The Psychology of Whiteness in the Workplace
by Brianna Miller
Expected drop: August/September 2025

Messy Magic Meals: A Cookbook
by Mikeila Miller
Expected drop: October 2025

My Planner, My Rules: Because My Vibes and Routines Matter
by Mikeila Miller
Expected drop: November 2025

The Possibility of Me:
A Mémoire in Three Movements

Brianna Miller

I am the kind of woman who authors her own life.
I am the one who wasn't before she was.
I am the Authress™.

On
Paper
PRESS

Eden Prairie, MN

Published by On Paper Press
An Imprint of On Paper LLC
Eden Prairie, MN
www.onpaperllc.com/on-paper-press

This book is a work of nonfiction based on the author's lived experiences. Some identifying details may have been changed to protect individuals' privacy.

Library of Congress Control Number: 2025914814
ISBN: 979-8-9995499-0-7

Cover design and interior layout by On Paper Press
First edition printed in the United States of America
First Edition
10 9 8 7 6 5 4 3 2 1

For permissions, inquiries, or media requests, contact:
onpaperpress@onpaperllc.com

Trigger & Content Awareness Statement
This memoir contains true stories and reflections that include themes of trauma, racism, sexual violence, adoption, grief, and personal transformation. These stories are shared with care and intention. Please move through this book at your own pace and honor your emotional well-being as you read.

Dedication

To little Brianna—
The girl who was overlooked, unseen, and too often discarded.
This is your story.
The one no one asked about.
The one they tried not to believe.
The one you survived, even when no one was watching.
You are carried on every page of this book.
You are no longer invisible here.

And to anyone who doesn't fit.
To the ones not included.
To the ones always on the edge of belonging—
I see you.
I wrote this so you could be seen too.

And to my Godchildren—
Sevan, Siniya, Antony & Archery & Nicherin, Harlem, and Amani—
I think of you every single day.
I send love and angels ahead of you, beside you, behind you.
I pray joy over your journey, strength for your becoming, health in
your bodies, and peace in your hearts.
May you always know you are loved—deeply, fiercely, and without
condition.
May you rise into the fullness of your names, your stories, your
power.
You are part of me. Always.

And to Uncle Mike—
The kindest man I've ever known.
You gave without expecting anything back.
You lived across borders, loved without hesitation, and saw
everyone as worthy.
You showed up for me, and for my children, without fail.

Dedication

I carry your spirit with me in how I see, how I serve, and how I love.
And even now, I feel you.
In butterflies that land on my shoulder out of nowhere.
In quiet moments when I need reassurance.
In sacred pauses when your memory shifts the air.
You are not gone.
You're just everywhere now.

And to my children—
Diamani, Abriana, Alyviah and Mikeila—
I love you more than you will ever know.
May you always know your worth.
May you always take up space.
May you always remember that your voice matters.
This is for you.
Because you matter.
And you will always be heard.

With Gratitude

This book exists because I wasn't alone.
Because people held me, challenged me, loved me, stayed with me.
Because someone believed I had something to say—even when I wasn't sure yet.

To the Ones Who Made This Possible
To the mothers who showed me what love could be.
To the sisters who knew without asking.
To the friends who stayed on the line until I could breathe again.
To the teachers who challenged my words but never silenced my voice.
To the ancestors who whispered: *Write anyway.*

I may not name everyone. But you're in this.
You're in the breath between these pages.

Thank you for holding me through it.

Thank you.

Epigraph

To carry the truth is to carry the weight.
To bear the ring is to walk alone.
And still—every day, I make progress.
There is learning in everything.

—Brianna Miller

Prologue: The Land of Isn'ts

I was never supposed to be here. Not because of biology or barriers or brokenness—but because I come from something that isn't. A place that can't quite be named, only known.
I come from something that isn't—not because it's nothing, but because it hasn't been written yet.

A whisper of what could be. A murmur of what hasn't been—yet.

It's not exactly a destination. More like a frequency. A wavelength. A whisper before the word. Somewhere between idea and incarnation. It's the space you imagine from before you're born—the one you write from, not to.
It's where everything lives before it becomes real.

It's the cousin of the in-between.
Both blurry. Both borderless.
Both unwilling to follow anyone's rules but your own.

This place shaped me.
A girl born from contradiction.
Named before she had a voice.
Called too much before she even arrived.

It's called *The Land of Isn'ts*.

I lived my early life like a question mark—trying to make sense of a sentence I didn't write.
But eventually, I did.

I learned that possibility isn't an outcome. It's a practice.

That you don't have to see the next step.
You just have to move like it's already there.

Prologue: The Land of Isn'ts

That you can be both terrified and ready.
Both unsure and unstoppable.

A wise woman once said, *"A possibility is something that isn't."*
And that's exactly what I am.
Something that shouldn't have been—based on statistics, silence,
and shame.
And yet.
Here I am.
And I remembered.

I remembered that I wrote this story before I got here.
That I was with God, with Spirit, with Source—
sitting at the edge of eternity, scripting a life from scratch.

I chose this body.
This name.
These parents.
These people.
This pain.
This power.
I chose it all—before it ever was.

Because that's what possibility is:
A blank page that hasn't been drawn on yet.
A crayon hovering in the air, waiting for the first stroke.
A story that doesn't exist until someone dares to write it.

I've always known I was writing my life as I lived it.
Even without words.
Even with trembling hands.
Even when the ink ran dry and I had to bleed onto the page just to
make the next sentence.

I've always known I was making this up—along the way.
Not like a lie.

Prologue: The Land of Isn'ts

Like a dream.
Like a vision I could see before it arrived.
Like a promise my soul whispered long before my body could
understand.

Some call it faith.
But this is deeper than belief.
This is *remembrance*.
Of what I am.
Of where I come from.
Of who I chose to be.

I come from the Land of Isn'ts.
Where nothing is real until it is.
Where dreams are not separate from destiny.
Where the Universe doesn't wait for permission—it waits for
participation.

And every time I speak something out loud, it gets legs.
Every time I believe in something no one else can see, it starts to
form.

That's the magic.
That's the risk.
That's the truth of living a life that didn't exist until you declared it.

Some say I'm lucky.
That I'm strong.
That I'm "resilient."
But this isn't luck.
This is design.

I show up.
And the next step appears.
I say it.
And the world shifts.

The Possibility of Me: A Mémoire in Three Movements

Prologue: The Land of Isn'ts

I imagine it.
And the path unfolds.

I've taught my children this too—
That their tongue is a crayon, and every morning they wake up with
a blank page.
That what they speak becomes shape and color and life.
And if they don't like the picture, they can start again.
Draw something new.

That's what I'm doing here.
Writing a new picture.
Making the unseen visible.
Living what wasn't—until it was.

The Possibility of Me isn't about what *is*.
It's about what refused to be erased.
It's about the lives we live before anyone gives us permission.
It's about becoming what you've never seen.
It's about building steps with your words and watching the ground
rise to meet you.

This book is a portal.
Into the Land of Isn'ts—
Where nothing is promised, and everything is still possible.
Into the breath between dreams and being.
Into the possibility of what you could be, if you believed yourself
enough to try.

And so here I am.
A possibility.
Made flesh.

This?
This is the story of how I made it real.

Author's Note

This story is raw. Maybe even untasteful to some. It is my truth.

I didn't write this for comfort.
Not for applause. Not for approval.
I wrote it because silence wasn't an option anymore.

If something in these pages resonates—beautiful.
Take what you need. Leave what you don't.
Or take nothing at all.

There's no assignment here. No lesson plan.
Just breath on paper. Just voice where there used to be silence.

If even one sentence gives someone permission—
the kind they never needed but were still waiting for—
then this book has already done its work.

This isn't a polished testimony.
It's a rupture. A reordering. A rites of passage. Me catching up to myself.
It is the story I wasn't supposed to tell—told anyway.

Now, I get to live.

I hope you find pieces of yourself here, too.
—Brianna

> *Journal Entry – 10/30/16, 7:03 p.m.*
> It feels like my life is starting today.
> Like it's the first day I've breathed.
>
> I am alive, ready for the next step.
> More ready than I ever knew or thought I would be.
> I'm breathing. I'm taking care of me.
> I cherish my existence and I'm stepping into it.
>
> I'm terrified.
> I don't want to ever be again where I was.
> However, I am grateful for the learning, healing, and growth.
> God has truly blessed me and kept me.
> I almost can't believe this is real.
>
> *Here I am world—it's really me—me for the first time.*
> *I'm here.*
>
> *And she writes...*
> *And it begins...*

Table of Contents

Table of Contents

Introduction: A Life Between the Lines

I've always lived between lines.
Between Black and white.
Between sacred and estranged.
Between mother and daughter, root and rupture,
silence and defiance.
Between being too much and not enough.
Between the story I inherited and the one I am now choosing to tell.

I didn't ask to live in the in-between.

it's where I ended up.
And it's where I've learned to breathe.

This book is not just a telling.
It is a mirror held to the parts of me no one ever fully claimed.
The girl who code-switched to survive.
The woman who raised children while still raising herself.
The mother who finally said: *enough.*
The writer who refused to wait until she had it all figured out.

You won't find a clean arc here.
But you will find truth.
In fragments. In fire. In faith. In full body.

This book holds the girl who didn't belong,
the mother who wondered if she could do it,
and the woman who—without fanfare—finally did.

This is not the story of someone who healed perfectly.
It's the story of someone who kept showing up anyway.

This is a life lived between lines.
And this is me.

The Possibility of Me: A Mémoire in Three Movements

MOVEMENT I: What Made Me

The story I was born into. The names I never chose. The truths I wasn't told.

The origin story no one else could tell.
This is the soil I was planted in.
Before I could name the world, it named me—
Mixed. Quiet. Angry. Different. Disruption.
I learned to survive before I learned to play.
I studied people before I studied books.
I became who I had to be.
And still—something holy in me refused to stay hidden.
This movement is memory and making.
It's the truth I wasn't supposed to speak.
It's the beginning I never got to choose.
But I'm choosing to write it now.

Chapter 1

What's In A Name

She Called Me Strength
My mother named me *Brianna* before I was born.

She chose it because it meant "woman of strength," and she told me I would need to have enough strength for the both of us. A white woman, unwed and pregnant with a Black child, facing down the violence and judgment of her own family—she knew what was coming. And still, she named me strong.

She reminded me of the meaning often. Especially when things got hard. She knew we'd need that word to hold us.

When she told her family she was pregnant, my uncle condemned her to hell for being a "nigger-lover." And yet—she named me. She raised me. She chose to walk through the fire. So yes, I believe there was love in it. Fierce love. Flawed, human, exhausted, and unstoppable love. I wonder what it felt like—to be treated like a disgrace for loving a Black man, for carrying me. But I think their rejection only made her stronger.

I used to think she named me strong because she believed in me. But now I wonder if she needed me to be what she couldn't. If my strength was her shelter—something to lean on when her own began to give out.

If it was a secret message filled with her hope inside.
I carried both of us for a long time.
I will always be my strength—and hers.

Being named strong can make people forget
That you bleed. That you ache.
I wasn't praised for needing care—
I was rewarded for surviving without it.

The World Didn't Fit Me
But the world didn't recognize what she named. Not in the mirrors they held up. Not in the places I tried to belong.

Back then, no one had my name. It wasn't on the gas station keychains. Not on the mini license plates. Never among the rows of trinkets you could spin at a truck stop. I'd search anyway—hopeful. But my name wasn't listed next to Amanda or Jessica or Sarah. I was already an exception. And I learned early that being real didn't mean being recognized.

People couldn't spell it. They couldn't say it right. And yet, it belonged to me so fully that I never questioned whether it fit. It fit me. It just didn't fit the world I was growing up in.
From the beginning, my name didn't belong to the world—it belonged to me.

She Built Me A World
She became the kind of mother who didn't just raise a child—she raised a resistance. She didn't try to make me fit into their world. She built one around me. One rich in culture and contradiction, survival and strength.

She surrounded me with brown and multi-everything. I had playdates with Indigenous kids, Hmong kids, Black kids, Muslim families, gay families. She sent me to language-immersion schools and took me to multicultural churches. She even took me to Africa. She taught me how to cornrow. How to make collard greens.

My mother didn't just raise me. She positioned me. To survive. To belong. To take up space in places they never expected me to enter.

The Names I've Been Called
fat.
bitch.
fat bitch.
white bitch.
dumb ass bitch.
fat ass white bitch.
slut.
nigger.
honkey.
monkey.
stupid.
lazy.
clueless.
too much.
a problem.
not enough.
a know-it-all.

But there was one name that always cut deeper.
Half-breed.
They said it like a diagnosis. Like my existence needed an explanation.
Even grown-ups said it.
I didn't have language for what I was—only for what I wasn't.
Not Black enough.
Not white enough.
I was made of both and neither,
and no one gave me language for that.
Not then.

Chapter 1: What's In A Name

I have been called all of these.
Whispered behind my back.
Shouted to my face.
Carved into the silences between who I was and who they wanted
me to be.

And then there were the ones they meant kindly.
Branna—my grandmother's soft tongue, Teisha and her girls' love.
Biriyani—the nickname from my South African family after a dish I
adored.
Bri—spelled *Bree* in my mind, sacred when spoken by the right
ones.
Not given, not demanded—just received.
And then there was the remix: Breezee or Eezee.
Or just E.

But even the soft names couldn't always soften the spaces I walked
through.

At Blake, they called me *Bri*—but it came with teeth, with edge,
with a reminder that I was passing through a place that didn't know
how to hold me.
There, I wasn't rich enough.
I wasn't white enough.
I wasn't enough.

I have carried all of these names.
Not because they belonged to me—
but because no one told me I could set them down.

And still, there was always a version of me
they couldn't touch.
A quiet witness.
A small girl watching it all,
surviving in silence.

To Little Brianna
Hey baby girl,
I see you.
Tucked under the table,
watching everything.
Quiet—but not because you don't have words.
Just no one ever really listened.
I want you to know—
you were never wrong for feeling it all.
The ache. The edge. The need to disappear.
You were never too much.
You were just unprotected.
Your name wasn't a shield then.
But it will be.
It will become a place to rest.
A name that knows how to hold you
even when the world cannot.
You did not break.
You bent, yes. You bent so far it scared you.
But look.
You're still here.
I see you.
And now—finally—
you're seen.

My Name Is Strength
People tell me I'm strong.
They say it like a compliment,
like a surprise.
Like strength is something I put on—
instead of something I am.

They don't know the half of it.

Chapter 1: What's In A Name

I have survived more than I have words for.
I have weathered storms that never made the news.
Carried losses that don't have gravestones.
Adapted so well it looked like ease.
It wasn't.

I moved forward because standing still would have broken me.
I smiled so others wouldn't feel uncomfortable.
I learned to speak gently when I wanted to scream.
And still—
I live.
Not because I want to be inspiring.
Because I refuse to disappear.

My name is everything to me.
It is the one thing I didn't have to grow into.
It fit from the beginning.
Not because I was ready—
because it was right.

I was born into strength.
Before I had language for it.
Before I had proof of it.
Before the world had a reason to believe it.

I carry it still.
In the way I keep loving.
In the way I keep writing.
In the way I choose myself—again and again.

I don't need anyone to call me strong.
I already know what I am.

I am it.

Chapter 1: What's In A Name

Strength was just the beginning.
There is so much more to me now.
And I'm still naming it.

And when I named Abriana—my Junyette (credit to Facesm),
mother of many nations—
I finally saw it.
She carried the world and made me want to survive it.
That's when I started stopping.
Stopping the cycle.
Stopping the lies.
Stopping being the punching bag, the ATM, the sex doll.
She didn't just make me a mother.
She made me *look at myself differently.*
Through her, I saw what I had survived.
What I no longer had to carry.
She opened the door—
but I walked through it.
And on the other side,
I found my strength.
Not hers.
Mine.

Chapter 2

To My Grandmothers

White Grandma
My maternal grandmother was my second heartbeat.

From the time I was 9 months old until I turned five, she was my daily caregiver. After that, I saw her weekly—until the day she died. She was my first safe place. The one who baked with me, sewed with me, taught me how to make pancakes and how to hold stillness.

She was quiet, but never weak. Her hands worked steadily and her eyes saw everything. She and her best friend Lorraine hosted the biggest garage sale on the block—it was an annual display of the weirdest trinkets and coolest knick-knacks. It was legendary. We'd price junk like it was treasure. I helped her sort through lives in cardboard boxes, folding stories back into shape.

She taught me the sacredness of small moments.

There was no television in her house. No chaos. Just old checkers games and quiet hymns, puzzles and garden soil, news radio and newspapers. And lots and lots of cooking. If I wanted to watch something, I had to go down to the basement—where Uncle Mike slept—and turn on a black-and-white TV no bigger than a first-generation Macintosh. One channel worked. Channel 2. I watched *Sesame Street* and *Mister Rogers* before my daily nap. The rest of the time, I was climbing trees, elbows deep in dirt, making doll clothes or baking something from scratch.

At church men sat on one side and women on the other.
There were no instruments. Just a pitch pipe, a hymnal, and voices
rising like a slow breath.
Blessed Assurance.
The Old Rugged Cross.
What a Friend We Have in Jesus.

That was the soundtrack of my childhood.

She died when I was 15.

Grandma of Mine – circa 1997, shortly after her passing

She taught me to accept everyone
      and to treat everyone the same way
She would take me to church in a hope,
      that I would find Jesus, even at such a young age.
She had never held a grudge with anyone that she knew
      and I never, ever knew her to be untrue.

We would make cookies as different holidays came
And she would stay inside and play with me when it would rain.
The patience she had and the warming songs she would sing
Taught me to remember this one important thing:

> *I'll love you forever even when it's good-bye*
> *And when I'm gone and you're lonely, just look to the sky.*
> *I will wave once or twice to send you a greeting from above*
> *Filled with fifteen years of happiness and love.*
> *I'll remind you that your heart will always be the same*
> *And if you look close enough all those precious memories still*
> *remain.*

Three months before she died, I met my father's family for the first
time.

Black Grandma

When my father called to ask if he could buy me a plane ticket to Alabama to meet his mother, I cried.

Because for the first time, I felt worthy of being introduced to the part of myself I had only imagined.

Even if my father didn't know what to do with all of me—my whiteness, my intellect, my softness—his mother welcomed me. She even stayed at my house in Minnesota when she visited.

She sent me gifts. She included me. On my 16th birthday, she sent me alexandrite earrings—the birthstone that represents the second gem of June. I later learned I share a birthday with *her* grandmother, which is why she was named Pearl, the first gem of June.

We didn't build a bond the way I had with my other grandmother, but we had something sacred. Something silent. We didn't need words. We were connected.

When she passed, I knew before the call came. I had a dream the night before—Granddaddy stretching his hand out to her. A gesture of welcome. Of reunion. My father called me the next morning. "Did you already hear?" he asked. I told him no. But I think he knew because he could hear it in my voice. I think she knew, too.

God in Two Faces

Both of my grandmothers were women of God.
Disciplined. Devoted.
Anchored in something deeper than doctrine.

They didn't drink. They didn't waver.
They were tenders of body and soul,
stewards of their homes and children.

One practiced her faith like the earth—
plain, steady, humble.
The other like royalty—
elegant, polished, dignified.
One was stoic. The other was soft-spoken.
Both were conservative, but in different languages.
One lived like a hymn.
The other dressed like Sunday.
One raised her children through stillness.
The other through style and steel.

And in them, I found two ways to be whole.
Two ways to be woman.
Two ways to be me.

To My Grandmothers
Thank you.
I haven't let you down.
Your presence and memory have carried me through this life.
And yes—I've seen you both since you left.
You know that.

To carry you inside me means I am already glorious.
You taught me how to keep a home and how to honor silence.
How to make pancakes, and how to lead with grace.
How to raise children—and how to raise a life from scratch.

I hope you see me now.
Still baking. Still soft-spoken sometimes.
Still finding God in quiet corners.
Your lessons live in my children's laughter,
in the way I fold my bed corners,
in the way I call on the name of Jesus when I pray.

I say your names when I need strength.
I call on you when the road feels too heavy.

Chapter 2: To My Grandmothers

I hear your songs in my breath when I exhale slowly and begin again.

You are both my angels.
And I have found peace.
And joy.
And freedom.

You did not leave me empty.
You left me full.

Chapter 3

The Skin I Speak

Between Worlds
They never tell you what it's like to live in skin that tells a different story than your soul.
They never prepare you for what it feels like when both of your worlds reject you.
I didn't learn about race in a textbook.
I learned about it in the pauses.
In the way white mothers scrunched their faces at me.
In the way Black girls looked me up and down.
In the way teachers expected brilliance, and then doubted my anger.

They called me articulate.
They called me "exotic."
They said I wasn't like "those other Black girls."
And not quite white enough to be one of them either.

And I—
I internalized it.
I tried to smile through it.
I split myself in pieces to make people comfortable.

My maternal grandmother met me at just a few days old and, almost relieved, exclaimed, "Oh! She is so light."
She used to take the colorful ballies out of my hair before church.
She'd braid down the braids, slick down the baby hairs.
She made me more presentable.

Less loud.
Less Black.

And yet—I never quite made it into whiteness either.
The first time I was called a nigger, I was in first or second grade.
It was a white boy around my age.
We were outside the babysitter's house.
She heard it. She scolded him. Then pulled him inside and left me outside on the steps alone.
I sat there until my mom came.
That's how I learned what isolation felt like.
That's how I learned my skin could make people disappear.

Too Much and Not Enough
At Blake, whiteness wasn't just the dominant culture—it was the oxygen in the building.
It was what you had to inhale to survive.
I wore the right clothes, I smiled at the right teachers, I answered the questions with too much precision.
And still, they looked at me like I was trespassing.

My father?
He always blamed my whiteness for everything between us that didn't work.
That was his excuse for every tension, every misunderstanding.
When I visited his family and offered to help do my cousin's hair, I was met with a look.
A tone.
A dismissal.
As if I had no business asking.
As if I didn't know.

Little did they know—
I was the hair guru in Minnesota.
I was the one helping all the white moms at church get their mixed babies' hair together.

I was the one moisturizing, detangling, braiding.
Teaching not just technique but history—telling the story of why
Black hair matters.

But Black people didn't always see me as part of them.
They questioned my voice, my clothes, my hair, my silence.
Black women never fully let me in.
Not to the circle. Not to the secrets.
I was included, but not initiated.

White people?
They raised me. They smiled and welcomed me and called me "fat"
behind my back.
Called me "ghetto" when I showed my rhythm.
Treated me like a curiosity, like a convenience.
Never all the way in. Never all the way out.

This is what I wrote during an in-class writing assignment in 11th
grade, trying to make sense of my identity:

In-Class Journal Assignment – 9/25/97 (Age 16)
Things About Myself I Would Like to Change—And One Thing I Would
Not

I know this will sound mean, but sometimes I wish I were either all
Black or all white. Yeah, being biracial has its benefits: I have two
totally opposite cultures, and I have a year-round tan. I also have a
lot to say when it comes to Black/white issues because I am both—
and I can see it from two points of view.

But that can get me in trouble, too. Black people will tell me I act too
white, and white people will always find something to mock me
about—whether it's the slang I use, what I put in my hair, the music
I prefer, or how I dance.

Chapter 3: The Skin I Speak

I get confused. I don't know how I'm supposed to act. Society considers me to be Black, but how do you *act* Black?

I am who I am—and it's hard for me to deal with either race.

Sometimes I wish I could live in South Africa, where mixed people have their own race. Maybe then people would understand me and why I do and say the things I do.
I could never ask for different parents, though—if that were possible. Except...I wish my dad would've been around more.

I'm blind, believe it or not, to both races too! I mean—race is beautiful. And God made me extra beautiful with two races. But it's not as easy as you think, especially with prejudice.
I don't fit in anywhere!

I'm also a very outspoken person—probably because I feel like I always have to defend myself. Maybe if I were one race, I wouldn't have that problem.

It's so controversial. And I don't want to sound like I want to disown either side of my heritage.

I don't even know which I would prefer: all white or all Black. Both have advantages and disadvantages.

It just makes life that much harder—and sometimes I can't deal with it. Especially at a predominantly white school. I wouldn't fit in at a predominantly Black school either.
So where do I go? Who am I? I don't understand.

I'm not African American—even though my ancestors were brought here from Africa. And I'm not Black—because I have white skin.
But to be politically correct, I'm African American.
Can't I just be American?

Chapter 3: The Skin I Speak

If I'm African American, then I have to be German, French, Swedish, Swiss *and* African American.

I don't know what else to say. I think I already said too much...

Everyone's Reflection, No One's Mirror
The truth is:
I have lived a thousand rejections in the same body.

I've lived in every position.
And in every one, I tried to hold the line together.
Tried to be the thread that doesn't break.

But even there, the contradiction found me.
My mom's side saw me as less than.
My dad's side treated me like a clueless white girl.
Too loud. Too soft. Too polished. Too unaware.
All of it—at once. Sometimes in the same day. Sometimes in the same breath.

I was everyone's reflection and no one's mirror.

I've fought to be seen and still blend in.
I've spoken, and they heard the wrong accent.
I've stayed silent, and they assumed I had nothing to say.
I've asked for advice—and gotten two opposite answers from each half of myself.

One Black. One white. Both certain. Both contradictory.
And I was caught in between.

I was the unspoken elephant in the room.
Too Black to be white. Too white to be Black.
I was the oxymoron no one wanted to name.
Because to name it would mean they'd have to face it.

The Narrative Flipped

To see me is to see a history that America has never healed.
Because when you see someone like me—with one Black parent and one white parent—you're not just seeing a "mixed" child. You're seeing a story. A reckoning. A rupture.
A story that, more often than not, began in rape or secrecy.
The legacy of a white woman who had to hide her lover—or a Black woman who never had a choice.
A body born from both love and violence, power and vulnerability, longing and betrayal—and forced to carry all of it without a map.

I carry the history of both.

And while people love to coo over "beautiful biracial babies," they rarely name what that beauty cost. They don't ask what had to be swallowed, hidden, or endured to make someone like me possible. They don't see the contradiction living in my skin.

Or maybe they do.

Because when people look at me, they don't just see my face—they see what they don't want to name. They feel what they've tried to forget.
Because to look at me is to remember:
Someone crossed a line.
Someone broke a rule.
Someone suffered for it.
And here I am—living proof.

But here's the part they really don't expect:
I am biracial. My mother is white. My father is Black.
But not in the way you've been taught to imagine.
Most people assumed my dad was some bum thug—couldn't provide, wasn't around, left us struggling.
They saw my mom and assumed she was the polished professional,

the strong single woman who came from money and held it all
down.
That couldn't have been further from the truth.

My white mother was the one on welfare.
She did look like that welfare mom they showed you in the media.
She worked three jobs, used food stamps, and clawed her way up
from receptionist to CEO—all without a college degree.

My Black father had his bachelor's, his master's, and eventually his
PhD.
He built a real estate empire, made millions, and once lived in a
house with a damn elevator in it, and another house with a pool
inside, right off the kitchen.

This is the truth I was born into.
The story no one expects.
The one that doesn't fit in anyone's brochure.

And it complicated everything I thought I knew about race, identity,
and belonging.
Because I wasn't just navigating two cultures—I was unlearning the
lies they both told about each other.

And about me.

Proximity, Power, and Perception
The layers only deepened as I got older.

When I was in middle school, my mother couldn't afford to live
anywhere near the neighborhoods of most of the kids I went to
school with. We lived in the same house all the way through high
school—one she bought all by herself when I was just 8 years old.
(Well, my dad was the realtor.)

Then, one day in high school, I was visiting my dad's house. I looked out the window and saw a classmate shoveling the walkway. That's when I realized—she lived in the neighborhood. My classmate. My dad lived in her neighborhood.

The kids at school were shook when they found out. After that, I was invited to parties. To houses. Into spaces I had never been in before. Because of proximity. Because suddenly, I wasn't just some ambiguous biracial girl with a single white mom and invisible Black dad—I was the girl with a dad in their zip code.

It was weird. Surreal. And wildly disorienting. Because my whole perception of what I thought was true—about race, class, and belonging—was flipped upside down.

My life has always challenged the story they're trying to brainwash us into believing.

I didn't just think about race—I *lived* it.
And I wrote about it, even when I didn't have all the answers.

The Other Side – 12th grade circa Spring 1999

"The grass is always greener
On the other side of the fence," they said.
I looked.
I compared.
I see no difference.

"Don't cross to the other side
of the fence," they said.
I wondered.
I waited.
I finally crossed.

"WHITES ONLY!"
I read.
But...I am not
White.

I searched:

"BLACKS ONLY!"
I read.
But...I am not
Black.

I searched:

Green grass I found
On the other side of the fence.
I looked.
I wondered.
I cried.

What side do I belong to?
Do I have to choose?
I can't go back now;
I can't go on.

"The grass is always greener
On the other side of the fence," they said.
"Don't cross to the other side," they said.

But I can't stay here.

More Proof Still Needed

In 2020, when George Floyd was murdered, I felt it in my body. It happened on the very corner where I spent so much of my childhood and early adulthood. I watched the videos—yes, the ones most people didn't. The ones where the ambulance turned the corner and sat on Park Avenue for at least ten minutes, using a machine inside the ambulance trying to bring him back. Trying to resuscitate him. But it was too late. We knew he was done for when he was still lying on the ground—under that officer's knee.

I took my kids to witness what was happening to our city. We sat outside the 3rd Precinct—cops in riot gear with shields and guns guarding the building. The streets were flooded with looters and rioters (not protestors—let's be clear on the difference), moving like it was the purge. No rules. No order. Just chaos, fury, and grief in motion. It was terrifying. It was glorious. It was hopeless and liberating, all at the same time.

And still, people tried to rewrite it.
Tried to soften it.
Tried to act like they didn't see what we all saw.
The caucasity (credit to Joel Martinez, 2012) and the niggnorance (that one's mine) that followed—online, in boardrooms, in church pews, at kitchen tables—was violent in its own way. A different kind of suffocation.
What more do you need?
White people are killing Black people in cold blood.
And getting away with it.
That's not up for debate.
That's not nuance.
That's reality.
And yet... here we are.
It's 2025.
And some folks are still pretending it didn't happen.
So I did the only thing I could.
I wrote.

Facebook Post – 5/29/20
(black is intentionally lowercase for this piece)

I am going to take a risk here: I am bi-racial, black and white (yet I identify as black/brown). Growing up, there were two distinct, separate parts of my life: a white one and a black one. I was introduced and raised intimately within the black community and the white community. I learned different ways to do things: to cook, to speak, hygiene, church etiquette, appearance, voice, roles, expectations, etc., many of which are unwritten and only understood when lived. To me there was never a right or wrong. Seeing two very distinct lives of a people (white or black), the similarity was that they were all trying to accomplish the same things in life (happiness, family, love, success) just differently #differentlythesame

I also understand that not ALL black people live like ALL other black people. I know that ALL white people do not live like ALL white people. Because I can pass (both white AND black), I have had the opportunity to experience a lot of different living within both black and white society. For example: poverty, wealth, rural, urban, conservative, liberal, pain, beliefs, religion, and so many more I cannot list them all. I have also traveled the world and I have experienced so so so many different kinds of people and cultures, and so I understand that we are not ALL the same.

For me, although I had an "in" with both blacks and whites, I was somehow never black-enough or white-enough. The black people in my life criticized me for being TOO white: my educated speaking, my skin tone, my ideas and beliefs, my physical shape, having too much, my dancing and singing, how I dressed, etc. The white people in my life criticized me for being "ghetto" or "hood," or one of the GOOD ones. They were critical of: my hair, my curves, my speech, my thoughts and beliefs, not having enough, my clothes. My grandmother even exclaimed the day I was born, "Oh, she is so light!"

My perspective into the dichotomy of my life has become a powerful tool. I have experienced racism from whites and blacks. If I walk down the street and come close to ANY man, I panic. I get followed around in stores, and anytime I see a police car I get paranoid. And I also have privilege. I should be a statistic: White single mother with a mixed child (they called her a nigger-lover), molested, domestic violence, bullying (lots and lots of bullying). But I also come from a long line of homeowners and business owners. I went to the doctor and the dentist regularly. I always had food to eat and clean clothes. We struggled, but I never saw it. I've always lived in stable housing. I went to the best schools. And I am one of the "lucky" ones, and only by God's grace did I not become a statistic.

I often find it hard to have a voice about race and inequality. I want to speak up on the injustices of black people, and against the system; yet many black people think I'm not qualified because I'm white and that my thinking is too radical or "new age;" and many white people get intimidated by my strong insights that they shut me down and put up the glass. I have been called both a nigger and a fat, white bitch.

What I ultimately see is that black people are at a disadvantage within our systems. Black and brown faces are disproportionately vulnerable to brutality, poor health, incarceration, violence, pandemics, poverty, poor education, death. We have a collective and historical trauma that impedes our ability to heal, and yes, slavery is the root of this. But I do not blame white people for slavery. I blame white people for perpetuating the injustices, and many times refusing to see the plight of black people. This is what we are screaming about, pleading about. SEE US! Recognize the imbalance and care about us enough as fellow human beings that you do something about it! This is the cry behind #BlackLivesMatter. LISTEN!

I do not agree with violence and rioting and looting-and know there are two different groups out there right now: peaceful protestors and opportunists. Yet, as I watch the city disappear, I can't help but understand the anger. If I were suffocated my whole life, I would fight my way to breathe. This is nothing new. ALL people have all risen up against governments ever since the beginning of time and all over the world (not just blacks and whites). There is injustice everywhere. However, right now, at this time, it is about Black and White. It is about race. It is about a city, a nation that continues to devalue black people! The systems MUST change!!

#GeorgeFloydsmurderwasthecatalyst #enoughisenough #thisisasymptom

---

I Am the Skin I Speak
Let me be clear—
I am not Black enough for you.
I am not white enough for you.
I am not enough for any box you try to put me in.

But I am me.

And that's not an apology.
It's a warning.
It's a celebration.
It's a sacred reclamation.

I am the skin I speak.
Brown, bold, biracial, battle-tested.

My skin speaks in code and contradiction.
It speaks in cornrows and private schools, in collard greens and academic scholarships.
It speaks Spanish and scripture, silence and survival.
It speaks grief and grit.
It speaks strength wrapped in softness, and softness sharpened by fire.

My skin speaks me.

And now I finally listen.

Chapter 4

What No One Saw

The Girl They Thought They Knew
They saw my smile.
They saw my grades.
They saw a girl who seemed okay.

But they didn't see the fire.

They didn't see how early I learned to scan a room—
for safety, for exits, for tone shifts in adult voices.
They didn't see how I read people before I ever read books.
How I memorized silence because it was safer than truth.
They didn't see the ache—a metronome of memory beneath my skin.
The way I laughed when I wanted to cry.
The way I overachieved so no one would notice I was unraveling.

They didn't see the exhaustion of code-switching.
Of carrying the right version of me into every room.
Of never being enough—but always being too much.
They didn't see me shrink when someone said,
"You're not really Black though," or
"No, she's not white, she's mulatto."
I learned to laugh—just enough to make it look like I wasn't hurt—
and then carry that moment like a stone in my mouth all day.

First Invasions

They didn't see the first time I was touched without consent.
I was three.
In the church basement.
Too young to know what violation was,
but old enough to remember.
To remember the taste of shame.
To remember the yellow blanket I tried to clean myself with.
To remember that silence was safer than asking for help.

They didn't see me outside
around the corner of the townhouses—
where I stood with my back against the brick wall
and with my pants down,
while the older neighbor boys took turns copping a feel.

They didn't see how I was caught.
Not them—*me.*

How I was the one punished.
How every time something was found out—
every time someone "told,"
I wasn't comforted.
I was beaten.

With belts.
With broomsticks.
With fists.
With the back of a hand.

With the wooden spoon—
I remember one whooping when she broke *every* wooden utensil in
the drawer.
She kept pulling them out one by one,
snapping them across my body
as I flopped across the kitchen floor,
praying there were no more to grab.

I remember her calling my grandparents to come get me because she was afraid she might kill me.

I was under five.

No one asked what they did to me.
Just what I did to deserve it.
So I learned to lie.
To hide.
To carry the shame for everyone else's hands.

They didn't see the other boys.
The cousins.
The way I learned sex before I learned boundaries.
How hands became currency.
How my body became a performance.
And how early I learned to disconnect from it.

Bruises and Barstools
They didn't see Billy.
His motorcycle.
His fists on my mom.
His wife, his girlfriend, his children.
The bar on Lake and Chicago named Sonny's
where I was the only child
playing pull tabs at age 6
and no one asked why.
They didn't see the road trip to Mississippi
or the hand that struck my head so hard
that ice water and butter knives became first aid.
They didn't see the little girl pretending to be okay
next to a man who called his violence love.
How my mom would reach for me and beg me not to leave the room
when he was there so she wouldn't be alone with him.

They didn't see how I was trained to read for danger.
To anticipate.
To disappear.

They didn't see what happened after he was gone.
How it didn't end—it just changed form.
How absence can still leave bruises.
How new men carried old patterns.
How love became a battlefield of contradictions:
be desired, be silent, be loyal, be afraid.

They didn't see the new set of eyes in the mirror—
not mine, but his.
Reflected in glass while I sat in bathwater,
small, naked, pretending not to notice.
The door wasn't closed all the way.
Maybe I didn't even think to close it—
I was a kid.
Maybe he pushed it open—
And I remember his eyes. I can still feel them.
My mom told him to stop.
He didn't.
So I learned to keep my eyes on the faucet.
To go still.
To count his footsteps like warnings.

The Record
They didn't see how I became a canvas for someone else's
unresolved past—
how pain painted itself on my skin,
how someone else's memories used my body as proof they hadn't
healed.
I held the brush for wounds that weren't mine.
I bore the colors of a rage I never earned.

Painted in bruises no one believed.
Because I still smiled.
Because I still functioned.
Because I still showed up looking like hope.

They didn't see the day he beat me senseless with a broomstick—
across my shins—
because I told him I hated him.

I hated him and his whole family.
And I said it out loud.

I grabbed the cordless phone,
ran up to my room,
and shoved the dresser against the door.
I called a classmate—
not a friend,
but someone I thought I could trust,
someone I thought might come save me.
I told her what happened.
I asked if she and her mom could come pick me up.
They didn't.

Days later,
they called me to the principal's office.
Child protection.
They took pictures of my legs—
the bruises were still there.
And when I got home,
the pastor was there.
He said he was disappointed
that I didn't come to him.
That I should have trusted him.

And then they said maybe—
maybe I had ruined the possibility of them ever adopting.

That he might have a record now.
That I had brought shame.
Not him.

Not the broomstick.

Me.

They didn't hear the silence that screamed through walls—
a silence so loud it rang in my teeth,
so dense it felt like suffocating in daylight.
No slammed doors. No yelling.
Just the kind of silence that says:
don't say anything, don't ruin everything.

Dressed in Effort
They didn't see how depression dressed itself as effort.
How I gained weight and disappeared into the squishiness.
How I stopped showing up to life
because showing up meant pretending.

They didn't see the teachers who said my writing was too dark.
Too grotesque.
Too heavy.
As if truth had to be gentle to be graded.

They didn't see how lonely it was to carry everything
and still get judged for dropping it once in a while.
Judged for being a single mother.
For getting an STD.
For choosing the wrong man.
For not being soft enough.
For being too soft.
For being short on the mortgage and asking for help.
Or for having a messy house.

They didn't see me.
Not all of me.
They saw what made them comfortable.

He Said He Loved Me
They didn't see the way "I love you"
turned into *you owe me.*
Into *you better.*
Into *if you don't, I'll find someone who will.*

They didn't see the way I shrank,
apologized, explained,
tried to stay soft so he wouldn't break me open.

They didn't see the night he punched me in the face
while holding a full set of keys—
and how when the pain hit, and the blood came,
I started crying.

And how his panic had him drag me out of the driver's seat,
throw me into the backseat,
on the floor—
and take the wheel
with no license,
no headlights,
going 70 in a residential zone
blowing through stop signs at 2am.

They didn't see my fingers
digging into the door handle
because I knew I might die that night.

They didn't see the tan suede coat I was wearing.
Or the way it turned bright red
as the blood soaked through.

They didn't see the moment
his paranoia started to settle,
how he pulled up to a dumpster
and threw the coat away.

They didn't see the scar above my lip
because they never looked that close.

They didn't see the shiver when no hand was raised.
The fear even in calm rooms.
The weight of being a girl
who never got to rest.

Let Me Be Clear
Some truths don't live in language —
But this one gets to.

So let me be clear.

What I've written in fragments —
The yellow blanket,
The bathtub,
The footsteps,
The hands,
The mirror —

It was rape.
It was molestation.
It was grown men and older boys
Taking what was never theirs.
Over and over
and over again.

In bedrooms.
In churches.
In cars.

In hotel rooms.

Some called it love.
Some were "just playing"
Some didn't call it anything at all.

But I remember.
My body remembers.
The shame.
The exposure.
The way time didn't stop, even when everything else did.
I carried the weight of those moments in silence.
I was too young to name them.
Too scared to say "no" and
too invisible for anyone to notice
the parts of me that were slowly disappearing.

I didn't have the words then.
But I do now.
And I won't dress this truth in soft language.

This is what happened.
And I survived it.

The Building I Live in Was Knocked Over – 1/14/08

The archaeologist who digs deep enough
Will find
My bones laid randomly
And will spend her time, losing her mind
Trying to redefine, why.
She will learn
About the burns
Pain, unearned
To an adult, a child turned

For her daddy
She yearned.
Brush that dirt aside
Let me hide, cover my eyes,
    Not wet, dried
She will see my naked bones exposed
Bare, pre-pubescent, adolescent
No clothes
She will know, "No!"
Quiet, alone
Put down the bones
Turn and walk home.

A Kiss in the Nursery

There was a boy.
A secret friend.
We talked on the phone for hours—whispers in the dark.
In public, he acted like he didn't know me.
But in private…
He was kind.
He made me feel like I mattered.
Like I wasn't invisible.

We were eight when he kissed me.
In the church nursery.
Just us.
No one watching.
I couldn't believe it was him.
The one everyone liked.
The one I had a crush on.
And he chose me.

Later, at church camp, the girls slapped me across the face—
again and again.
He stood between us.
Told them to stop.

And for a moment, I was protected.
Seen.

I didn't have words for it then.
But later, I found a poem,
written in the voice of Gary Soto.
And I used his rhythm to write my own memory.
It was fictional, in part.
But the feeling?
The feeling was real.

Coke – **10th Grade circa 1996-1997**
in the style of Oranges by Gary Soto

The first time I kissed
A boy, I was seven
Trembling, and held back
By my nervous conscience.
January. Chimney smoke
Resting upon my lips, the
Sound of ice skates scraping on the ice like
Nails scraping a chalkboard,
Beating, my heart inside me, then stopping
As I reach to pull
Open the door to the church, the
One whose water fountain always dripped
Night and day, to any rhythm.
I stayed to myself, until
He came out walking
His walk, hair slicked back
With grease. I fidgeted,
Took his hand, and led
Him to the door, across
A well lit parking lot and a row
Of newly tossed garbage,
Until we were breathing

Before the corner store. We
Entered, the squeaky hinge
Bringing a man
From behind the counter.
I turned to the soda
Stacked like pillars
And asked if I could have a Coke—
Grin upon his lips, a twinkle
In my eye. He felt
For a dollar in his pocket,
And when I lifted my Coke
He didn't say a word.
He took the dollar from
His pocket, then my Coke,
And set them cautiously on
The counter. When I looked up,
His eyes met mine,
And held them, kindly,
Like a mother
Holds her baby.

     Outside,
A snow plow rolled past,
Tree branches cracking like
A whip on a horses skin,
My boy took me in his arm
And kissed my lips,
But released quickly
As our childhood frightfully grew
To a stage of adolescence.
I went into my pocket
And pulled out my Coke
That, from a distance
Someone might have thought
My heart exploded through my chest

And landed into my hands.

He was my friend in the shadows.
The boy who kissed me in secret.
Who saved me, quietly, when it mattered.
We never had a story that lasted.
But in that moment,
he gave me something no one else did:
a softness that stayed.

My Receipts
What no one saw
was how much I was carrying.
The rage. The ache. The knowing.
The humor I used to deflect.
The silence I weaponized.
The way I turned survival into rhythm.
The way I made trauma look like talent.
The way I kept going—
even when I was breaking.

No one asked what it cost.
No one asked what I lost to seem so "composed."
No one asked what I dreamed about—
because dreaming wasn't expected of girls like me.

But even in that breaking,
there were moments.
Moments that weren't loud or lasting—
but they stayed.

They stayed like a soft light in the corners of my memory.
They stayed like a warmth that couldn't be taken.

And maybe that's what saved me.

Not the fixing. Not the fighting.
But the fragments of tenderness.

The shadows where someone saw me.
Even if no one else did.
And so I dreamed anyway.

I dreamed of being held without being fixed.
Of being heard without explaining.
Of being seen without proving.
Of being all of me—
the joy and the grief, the ache and the laughter,
the brilliance and the shadow.

And somewhere deep inside—long before the coaching and the
conferences and the titles—
I knew I was more than what they saw.
Even when I didn't have the words, I had the knowing.
The knowing that I was layered.
That I was light and shadow.
That I was rage and reverence.
That I was something no one had ever made room for.

And now?
Now I write her back into the story.
The girl they missed.
The woman they never expected.
The voice that never needed permission.

Because what no one saw
became the part of me
that refused to disappear.

Chapter 5

Tiles and Blood

The Girl in The Bathroom
The bell rang, but I didn't move.

I sat through class like a ghost—the kind that still smiles when called on.
The kind that laughs at jokes that aren't funny.
The kind no one notices is slipping away.

In 7th grade science class, we built cars—shaved axles, tightened wheels.
Each of us was given a razor blade to trim parts with.
I kept mine.
Because I needed something sharp to match how everything inside me felt.

That day, I walked into the bathroom—the old one, before the school remodel.
White tile. One stall. A single sink.
It looked almost sterile.
Almost holy.
The cleanest place I could find to unravel.

I didn't even make it to the stall.
I dropped to the floor.

Everything started spinning.
My hands shook. My vision blurred.
I couldn't form a single word.

I didn't want to die.
I just wanted the ache to stop.

And in that moment, my body gave me an option:
silence and stillness.

No tears.
No screams.
Just a girl pressed against tile,
trying to disappear from the inside out.

There was one high window in that bathroom.
Too high to reach, but not too high to see the sky.
The tips of trees swayed just outside the glass.
The clouds looked like they didn't know where they were going
either.

The light was soft. Pale. Gray-blue.
And for a split second,
I remembered how to breathe.

Then the door opened.
Footsteps. A backpack hit the floor.

"Brianna? What are you doing?"

It was Molly.
Her voice wasn't sharp.
It wasn't panicked.
It was calm. Even.
With just enough disappointment to cut through the fog.

That's what stopped me.
Not fear. Not shame.
But the fact that someone saw me—fully—and didn't look away.

She didn't try to fix me.
Didn't make it about her.
Didn't sound the alarm.

She just *stood there*.

And I stopped.

Left Standing Still
Some days the violence was loud.
Most days, it was subtle.
A seat not saved.
A look.
A rule that only applied to me.

I carried every insult like a new weight.
And I learned how to walk with it without limping.
That's how I survived—
Straight-backed, silent, spinning inside.

I was the child with questions and imagination and bright eyes—
but always being told to sit still, speak less, behave better, be
smaller.

Age five.
I was blamed for spraying water on another girl's hair. I didn't do it.
Still got in trouble.

Another home.
Locked in basements.
Mouth washed out with soap.
Told I had ruined Santa—though I still believed.

American Girl dolls lined up on the table, but I was never allowed to touch them.
The other daycare kids played freely.
One girl was always kind to me.
But kindness had limits.
And so did I.

Fourth and fifth grade.
Church camp.
The Black kids hit me.
Slapped me over and over again across the face.
Laughed at me.
I was the wrong kind of Black girl.
Too soft. Too smart. Too me.

Same time.
Same grade.
I wore boots another girl had from the free box.
Mine were bought by my mom.
They tripped me.
Beat me up on the playground.
They laughed while I lay there.

Eighth grade.
I remember eating lunch every day in Mrs. Bjork's room with Jolie.
I love that girl.
We saved each other.
That room was our refuge.

Tenth grade.
They drew cartoons—cows, pigs—
Wrote my name across their bodies.
Stabbed them with pencils when the teacher turned away.
It was funny to them.
They were laughing.
I was shrinking.

Senior year.
The trip was planned without me.
Not one person told me.
My mom offered to pay for the entire room—
Two beds for four girls.
Me on the floor.

They still said no.

Even family did it.
On both sides.

So I learned to disappear.
To smile on cue.
To overperform.
To carry shame in silence.
To stop dreaming.
To stop expecting.
To stop.

Disappearing as Refuge
The tile remembers me.
So do the basements.
So do the boots.
The cartoons.
The bathrooms.
The rules I never made but always paid for.
The trees I used to climb.
The books I lost myself in.
The mirror I practiced my face in.

My soul remembers softness.
My spirit remembers who I was before the bruises.
That part of me stayed untouched.

Unbroken.
Whole.

I protect her now.
The girl beneath the armor.
The light they tried to dim.

There are versions of me I buried
just to make it to the next day.
I mourn them now.
I forgive them, too.

I didn't know it then,
but I had already crossed into the in-between space.
The place where I'd learn to see without being seen.
The place that made me sharp and silent and whole.

And finally—
after all that noise,
I exhale.

Fully.
Finally.
At last.

And She Spoke Anyway

Here are some poems I wrote in middle school
circa 1994-1995.
When I didn't know how to say what I felt—
I wrote.
When I didn't feel safe—
I wrote.
When I was tired of holding secrets—
I gave them shape on paper.
Each one is a thread

in the tapestry.
A breath I wasn't allowed to
take out loud.

Friends

joyfully playing
always there
people who
will always care

Him

He's furry gray and white;
he's there for me day and night.
He can play cards, catch, and more
and when I come home
he's waiting for me inside the front door.
I love him and he loves me
Together me and him make a wonderful "We!"

Untitled 1

I wish the earth to be more peaceful,
the wind to whisper togetherness
and all the childish doings
to rise above us.

Untitled 2

Look at the difference!
Compare these two worlds
to the pain I bare—
this hurt never fixed;
this heart always broken—
then judge me

Never Again

Never again will I let it go
Never again will it leave
Never again will I make a foe
Never again will I receive

Never again will I try
  or be foolish and ruin my life
Never again will I walk away
Never again will I lie

I will never open to the outside world
No one understands my place
All these things I must hide
And cover my shameful face

Robin Red-Breast

Little robin Red-Breast
sleeps by the old chest
near pussy cat
a very old pest

Pussy cat the old pest
peers upon Robin's breast
then makes a big leap
to rip open Robin's chest

As the cat draws near
the poor bird does hear

He awakens quite fast
then lets out a horrid gasp

Pierced in his Red-Breast
while fighting for his own nest
never to awaken
from his long rest.

The Sun Set

As the sun takes a rest
in a bird like nest,
To give the other morn
before the night is born;
Soon it will come again and give the light
while the other morn is night

Unfinished Seasons

Spring

The air was cold and wet,
the sky was dark,
yet bright,
the sun was waking over the sky
and settled right over my head;
The wind came,
hollowing a tune,
a lullaby,
it blew the tree branches asleep;
A Robin, or was it a sparrow,
came to sit upon the branches scratchy fingers,
and fall asleep;
A tear came trickling down
from the big puffy shadows
that swim in the sky,
 and landed on my toe;
It sprinkled,
it poured;

The sweet smell of dawn was tickling my nose,
the taste of the air was upon my lips;
The sky winked at me,
my heart melted into a blood-red soup—
SPRING!!
It's here.

Autumn

Autumn's a various season.
No two autumns the same,
  Comes in warm,
    children laughing and playing
    leaf piles big enough to clench your soul;
  Comes in a breeze with a fresh scent, a piercing
    hollow windy cry to scream a deathly vow;
  Comes in cold, snow falling slowly, sewing a blanket
    to cover nature's bed;
  Comes in furious, storms swaddling the branches of
    the trees in a solemn rhythm;

You see your breath disappear in a faint white mist,
  that floats up to the foggy heavens…
    Bringing upon death;
    Making way for new life.
  Overpowering the souls of worthless hearts
  And devouring the plethora of unwanted faces in
    a sudden gush of sunshine.

The paucity of hopes shattered and washed away by the
  fearsome rains that fall so heavily;

    Wet;
    Warm;
    Cold;

Autumn.

Untitled 3

Where the heart is cold,
where the feelings are hurt,
where all the triumphs are broken,
Brianna is

Untitled 4

Why was I always beaten,
always threatened,
always crying,
forever ashamed

Chapter 6

Mama Wasn't Soft, But She Was Gold

The Weight I Carried
My mother wasn't soft.

She didn't say the right things, not always.
She didn't sugarcoat or tiptoe.
She wasn't gentle in the ways white motherhood was painted on TV
screens or in Hallmark cards.
But she was gold.
Solid. Heavy. Unmistakable.
She held value that didn't glitter—but grounded.

She raised me like I was made of both fire and glass—
tough enough to withstand the world,
fragile enough to feel it deeply.

She didn't have the privilege of coddling.
Not with the world we were walking into.
Not with a child whose skin would be questioned before it was
embraced.

She always says, "I love you."
And she always said, "Be careful."
She didn't always hug me.
But she always showed up.

She gave me life.
She chose me.
And I felt that truth in her bones—even when I didn't always feel it in her tone.

There were times I wondered if she resented what I represented:
A daughter who made her a single mom.
A daughter who made her family turn on her.
A daughter who made everything harder.

I carried that weight, the unspoken one, the one that whispered: *You owe her.*
And maybe I did.
Not because I caused her pain—but because she carried it anyway.

Mommy Told Me – 8th **grade circa 1995**

Mommy told me I was a child of the sun,
And that when it snowed the angels were having pillow fights,
She told me that whenever it thundered God was bowling
And when there was lightening God was hitting strikes.

Mommy told me I was a child of the sun,
When I asked she told me the sun was my daddy
And when I got a suntan
She told me he was shining his love on me.

Mommy told me I was a child of the sun,
And that I was lucky to have yellow skin,
She told me I was special and people would call me names
She told me people would call me "Nigger."

Mommy told me I was a child of the sun.
And that I had to have strength
And no matter what anyone said or did
I'd always be the same.

Mommy told me I was a child of the sun,
And she was a child of snow,
She told me my real daddy was a child of the sands
And that my friends came from a rainbow.

Mommy told me I was a child of the sun,
And that I forever would be
She told me to never want to be something else
And she told me I should never ever try to change.

Doors She Opened
She gave me exposure.
Modeling. Piano. Violin.
Private school. Church camp. Radio. Television. Travel.
Spanish.
My first business trip—to Hawaii—alone at age twelve.
She found a way to open every door.

She built a life that didn't just include Blackness—it celebrated it.
She gave me Park Avenue Church—
a spiritual home where gang members, elders, professional ball
players, elected officials, police officers, community activists and
neighbors sat side by side.
It was multicultural. Real. Radical.
Prince got married there.
I found God there.
And community.
And joy.
Because of her.

Expectations & Disappointments
She believed in me.
She had expectations.
High ones.
She expected me to become *someone*—

And when I didn't become the version she imagined,
the disappointment came in quiet waves.

She showed me how to lead, how to serve, how to give.
She helped me with school projects.
Even wrote a paper for me once when I panicked.
She was generous with others—and, in her way, with me.

But I didn't always feel seen.

Time was sacred to her.
3:00 p.m. meant 2:45 p.m.
And my pace didn't match hers.
Even when I tried.

Sometimes, I wanted more grace than she could give.
I wanted presence more than performance.
But she was holding the weight of both our worlds.

The Moments That Glowed
There were moments that glowed.

Like when we were at the Blue Top Inn,
at the auction for Orlan and Mary's things.
She was talking to family and said she didn't have many friends—
then paused, looked at me, and said:
"Well, I consider Brianna my friend."

She probably doesn't remember it.
But I do.
I felt seen. Not just as a daughter, but as a person.
And I carry that with me.

I remember curling up next to her, watching Lifetime movies
before I turned eight.
Just being near her.

I remember the gentleness in those years.
It's a softness I've missed.

I remember her holding my hand after the Code Blue.
When she almost died—right in front of me.
And I couldn't move.
When it was over, she reached for me.
And I knew.
I mattered.
I was her comfort.
I just hadn't known it before.

She was there for my births.
Even the "births" I initiated.
Each one.
She stayed.
She held space.

She never quit.

The Woman She Was
She taught me how to show up.
How to try new things.
How to move forward even when the world gave you reasons not to.

She taught me how to be a woman who does not fold.

I don't believe she meant to ever hurt me.
And I no longer hold her responsible for what she didn't know how to give.
She was surviving, too.
And doing it well enough to teach me how to do the same.

She didn't always say she was proud.
But I know she is.

And I am proud to be her daughter.

My Mother's Rose (excerpt) – *circa* 2000, age 19

My mother is that rose—
that beautiful red rose
standing in the center of my world
this rose grows in my heart
wherever I go
and it is there doing
whatever I do
... and all that I learned from that rose
it will grow in me
and spread to my children
and their children
and even more children to come
But it started from that red rose
that beautiful
strong and
brave
red rose...
my mother's rose.

Backbone Over Softness
She didn't hand me softness.
She handed me a backbone.
She handed me questions that didn't have answers.
She handed me a mirror, then dared me to look.
She handed me herself—unfiltered, unpolished, unafraid.

I didn't know it then,
but I was watching a woman invent herself in real time.
Getting her degree from the University of Hard Shit.
Working late, crying early, fighting when it mattered,
and resting only when no one was watching.

So no, she wasn't soft.
Softness isn't what saved me.

She was gold.
And gold doesn't bend.
It just shines harder
when you polish it with truth.

Journal Entry – 1/15/20
My mom is wise beyond anything I had even believed. I never gave her much credit, and I am hurt that I disregarded her so. This is a turning point for me - beyond her actions, but seeing her soul. She is magnificent!

When I Saw Her in Me
For years, I swore I'd never be like my mother.
I didn't want her pain, her sharpness, her silence.
I didn't want to raise my kids in a house that felt like walking on eggshells or disappointments.

But the more I healed, the more I began to understand her.
Not just as the woman who raised me,
but as a woman who *wasn't finished being raised herself.*
I saw how much I carried that wasn't mine—and how much I judged before I understood.
And in that reckoning, I stopped trying to undo her.
And I started to meet myself.

Class Assignment – 9/22/13
Today I met my mother. In my experience, an unsure-of-herself woman trapped in her childhood criticisms, seeking approval from everywhere, but through her own interrogation. I met a woman with the purest of intentions of having a family and raising her children. I met a woman lost in her regrets, finding in every moment the opportunity to regain self-approval, mimicking what she thinks

looks good that others do and say. Today I met my mother. A woman intending to love and care for her children, spending a score of her lifetime concentrated on her shortcomings and self-perceived inadequacies.

"She felt guilty like all mothers who blamed themselves when terrible events happen to their children." *(Angelou, 2008)*

Today I met me.

I never thought I would find my mother when I looked in the mirror, "…my mother was a great example of everything I didn't want to be." *(Reichl, 2009)* The last person I wanted to see was the dictating bureaucrat who was never satisfied; the verbally degrading wake-up call and goodnight kiss. I was sure I would never be her. But when I looked in the mirror and saw her staring back at me as me…"She was thoughtful, more self-aware and much more generous than I had ever appreciated." *(Reichl, 2009)*

She was not who I knew at all—a faint memory of a woman that disappeared in her marriage and her career. I found her again, in the mirror. I saw her running and playing and scraping her knees. I saw her disciplined by her parents and ridiculed by her peers. I saw her see me take my first steps and fall and get back up. Through the wrinkles reflecting back, I realized: "We carry accumulation of years in our bodies and on our faces, but generally our real selves, the children inside, are still innocent and shy as magnolias." *(Angelou, 2008)*

She is a daughter, too. Not just my mother.
I am relieved.
Today I get to be me.
I get to see me.
I get to see me as my mother and my mother as me.
And I am still me.

Chapter 6: Mama Wasn't Soft, But She Was Gold

Dear Mom,
You are my hero.

You chose me—even with all the mess, the risk, the cost of bringing me into this world. You loved me the best way you knew how. You gave me a life of doors I didn't yet know how to open, of opportunities that many never get to dream.

You sacrificed for me.
You made hard decisions.
You did what you thought was right.

And it wasn't always enough.
I wasn't always protected.
I didn't always feel seen.
I wasn't always safe.

But I don't hold that against you.

Because I know—deep in my bones—that everything you did was for my best. I know your intentions were anchored in love, even when your words were sharp, even when your silence felt like distance. Even when you didn't know what to do and had to make it up on the spot.

I love you, Mom.
To the depths. To the crevices.
To the places inside me that only exist in my knowing.

Thank you—for your fire.
For your fight.
For your presence.
For your gold.
I see you.

Thank you for what you did

to make me possible.

All my love,
Brianna

Chapter 7

Black Father, White Ghost

Infamous Offspring

I always knew who my father was.
He wasn't invisible.
He was known—by everyone, it seemed.
What I didn't understand was why knowing him never felt like being his.
Even though I don't carry his last name,
I carried the space he left behind everywhere I went.

My father was a legend in Minnesota.
Say his name, and people straightened up.
Even now, people hear who my father is and treat me differently.
People had stories, memories, inside jokes.
I had absence.

They knew him better than I did.
And that never made sense to me.
He lived near me my entire life—probably never more than 20 minutes away.
But proximity isn't presence.
And I learned to hold onto pieces.

The Dinosaur

One of my earliest memories:
I'm three, at the top of the stairs, wrapped in a towel.
He's there—part myth, part man.

Chapter 7: Black Father, White Ghost

He came to my third birthday party at McDonald's.
Then he disappeared again.

When I was five, I had my tonsils and adenoids removed.
I remember waking up from anesthesia—groggy, confused, sore.
And there it was.

A dinosaur.
Green like peas with a bright yellow belly.
Made of this strange, pleather-like material—shiny but soft, with
multi-colored felt spikes down its back and tail.
That's the first thing I saw when I opened my eyes.

I asked for my mom.

"Where did this come from?"
They told me: your dad brought it.

And somehow, that was enough.
I didn't need to see him to feel the impact of that gesture.
That dinosaur became proof. A presence.

And then—I saw him.
He was really there.
In the hospital room.
For me.

It didn't happen often, but it happened that day.

And I held onto that dinosaur for years—through moves, through
heartbreak, through growing up.
Its little pleather belly pressed to my own when I needed something
to hold.

Eventually, it got lost in a move.
Still, I never forgot that moment.
Because that day, even if only for a few minutes,
he showed up.

And that mattered.

I didn't see him again until I was seven.

Two of my sisters were living with him by then.
Only one of them spoke to me.
She treated me like her baby.
Let me sleep in her room. Did my hair. Watched over me.

The other didn't speak to me—not then.
She was the one with the waterbed.
And the one behind the wheel, learning to drive.
My dad sat in the passenger seat.
Me and my other sister rode in the back.
Boy George played on the radio:
"Don't Take My Mind on a Trip," and
Milli Vanilla promised we could *"Blame it On the Rain."*

I got my hair done by Michael.
Got snuck into a teen club.
Hid under someone's feet when the cops pulled us over.
I called aunties on the phone.
Tried to figure out who I belonged to.

The Bruise That Stayed
When I was eight, I asked him why he wasn't around more.
He looked me in the face and said, "Because you whine too much."
Said his lifestyle wasn't for kids.

I was eight.
Trying to understand why I didn't have what other kids did—

why I couldn't count on him to show up.
And that was his answer.
Not "I'm sorry."
Not "I love you."
Just blame—placed on the smallest version of me.

I didn't cry.
I nodded, swallowed it, and decided not to ask again.

And that bruise—it stayed.
It settled in a quiet part of me.
The part that learned early not to expect too much from men.
The part that took silence as standard.

I didn't forget it—
Not then.
Not later, when someone else used the same excuse
to walk away in my early twenties.
Said the exact words:
"Because you whine too much."

And suddenly, I was eight again.
Small.
Unworthy.
Wounded in a place that didn't bleed—but never really healed.

It's a wound that knows how to keep quiet.
And it still throbs.

Billboard Father

I'll never forget the day my mom pointed to a billboard.
"That's your father," she said.

There he was—*my* dad.
Larger than life.

Chapter 7: Black Father, White Ghost

His face, his business,
looking out over the street like a monument.

It made me proud.
I told everyone.
Even watched for it
from the school bus window.

It was proof.
That he existed.
Which meant *I* existed.
That I came from somewhere.
That I wasn't just made up.
That I was *real*.

But that wasn't the only place his image lived.
For years, he was on the back and inside front covers of the
Minnesota Black Pages—a full-page ad.
It was the official directory of Black-owned businesses in the
state. Well-respected. Widely distributed.

And there he was. Year after year.
Polished. Powerful. Public.

I used to bring those magazines to school.
Held them up like proof.
"This is my dad."
Because I needed people to know he existed.
To know I wasn't fatherless, even if he wasn't showing up for me.

He wasn't at the performances.
Or the award nights.
Or the field days.
But I had the page.
And for a long time,
that was all I had.

I was proud.
And I was also trying to prove something—
To them. To myself.
That I was chosen. That I belonged to someone.
That I mattered to him in a way the ad seemed to promise.

Ten Dollars in Change

When I was twelve, my brother stayed with him for the summer.
He worked at McDonald's.
We went to visit.
My dad paid in coins—pennies, nickels, dimes.
Not because he didn't have the money, but because he was teaching us a lesson in frugality, he said.

Ten dollars in change, scattered across the counter like it didn't matter.
My brother was working the register.
I was standing there staring at the hundreds of coins.
And for different reasons, we were both embarrassed.
Not by the cost—
but by the moment.

He looked like wealth in the magazines.
Like power.
But in that moment—at that counter—
I saw something else.
A lesson maybe.
Or a man unsure how to be a father
when the cameras weren't watching.

Claimed, At Last

When I was fifteen, I needed his signature to get my passport for Africa.

He signed.

Chapter 7: Black Father, White Ghost

Then he offered to take me to Alabama for Thanksgiving to meet his family.

My grandmother.
My Granddaddy Tamp.
His sisters. Their families.

I already knew I had three siblings.
Before the trip, I learned there were two more—one older than me, one younger.
Six in total.
Each of us with a different mother.
I was the only one with a white mom.

He told me it had once been shameful to bring me home.
But that year, he did.
He bought the plane ticket.
Paid for everything.
And for the first time, claimed me out loud.

During that trip, one of my cousins ran up and jumped into his arms.
He laughed. Picked her up. Spun her around.
He was never like that with me.
And I never stopped noticing the difference.

But something shifted after that.
Not just between us—within me.

For the first time, I saw Black people in a way that had never been presented to me before:
family-oriented, financially successful, respectful, and educated.
They were full of warmth and excellence—without apology.

I began to question my definition of Blackness.
To unlearn the stereotypes I had swallowed from both sides.

And I started to embrace the strength and beauty of my entire family—
and myself.

That trip didn't erase the past.
It didn't fix what had been missing.
But it gave me a glimpse of who I came from—
and what I could grow into.

He started showing up more after that.
Not just in person—but in ways I didn't expect.
And I started rooting myself not just in pain—
but in possibility.

He Showed Up

He was there when my mother's mother died. Quiet, respectful, present— even when my stepdad cornered him, chastising him for his absence, for everything he hadn't been. My dad didn't argue. He took it. He endured the moment and stayed for as long as he could take it. That mattered more than anyone knew.

And he still came back three weeks later when my grandfather died.

He walked me in the grand march at prom— a moment I didn't even realize I needed until it happened. He stood and watched the plane take off on my first trip to Europe. He bought me a blue jacket from Gap for that trip— simple, perfect. I wore it like armor. It meant I was seen.

He gave me a room in his house—the one with the pool inside, right off the kitchen. I never slept there, but it was mine. It felt like being chosen. Like there was space for me in his world. Not just a visit. A room. A place.

He took me to New York to visit family for Christmas. All his siblings and their families were there. My grandparents and some of my other siblings too. And I was there. Included. Present. Belonging, even just for that moment.

We started eating at restaurants together. Talking. Laughing. I worked for him and with him. He let me see him in his element— how he moved, how he led. And I started to know him not just as "Dad," but as a man.

And then— he came to the hospital when my son was born. That was major. It was the first birth he'd ever attended. He walked beside me up and down the hallway during early labor. My mom was there too. At one point, they both started laughing—hard. My dad had just realized I was about to push a whole watermelon out of my body, and all he could compare it to was his worst-ever bowel movement.

I laughed too. Even in the pain.
Because somehow, they were there.
Together.
For me.
And he stayed.
That meant more than I can explain.

Something Softened
Only recently, something softened.

He's embraced my children.
Fully. Without hesitation.

The things he once would've judged—he's let go.
Once, he said,
"I don't care what you are. Just be a rich one."

I understood what he meant.
That was his version of love.
And in that moment—I received it.

No More Waiting

For years, I thought I was the reason he didn't stay.
If I had been quieter, easier, brighter, Blacker—maybe it would've been different.
Maybe I would've been enough.

But I don't carry that anymore.

His absence shaped me.
But it doesn't define me.

I'm not waiting anymore.
Not by the window.
Not by the phone.
Not in the hollow places where little girls ask, "Why not me?"

He wasn't invisible.
He wasn't mine in the way I needed him to be.

And still—

I am.

I'm not the daughter he raised.
I'm the daughter who rose.
And that is enough.

Dear Dad,

There was a time I carried so much pain.
Not just from what you didn't do, but from what I thought it meant about me.

I was angry. I was hurt. I didn't understand why your presence was something I had to prove.

But you weren't gone to hurt me.
And when I let go of that belief—
when I stopped needing the past to be different—
I made room for who you are now.

We've spent the last twenty years, give or take, building something real.
You've shown up as the father I didn't have back then—
not perfectly, but fully.
When I let myself listen, your wisdom reaches me.
And it guides me.
That means more than I ever said out loud.

I love that I can call you now—and you'll answer.
Or you'll call me back.
I love that I can walk into your celebrations and family know who I am.
That I can sleep in your home when I visit Montgomery.
That I am welcome.

I love that you call me your daughter.
That you call me *Little Bit.*
That you care about me and my children—
not just that we survive, but that we end up well-off, well-loved, and whole.

And honestly?
That's all I care about.
Because at this point in my life—
that's what matters.

I love you, Dad.
For what was.
For what wasn't.
For all that still is.
And for what is to come.

Love,
Brianna

Movement I Summary: *What Made Me*

I was shaped by silence, scarcity, and stories that weren't mine.
But I also carried a pulse—a rhythm—that said I am more.
The ache did not erase me. The absence did not define me.
Even then, possibility lived in me.
Even then, I was writing toward freedom.
Now I see: what made me didn't own me.
It taught me to listen deeper. To see sideways. To name what others bury.
That's where I began.
I carried everything they gave me—stories, silences, expectations.
I made it look easy. I made it look like mine.
But inside, I was splitting. Stretching. Starving.
I had outgrown the world I was born into.
But I didn't yet know how to build my own.
So I wandered.

Welcome to the in-between.

MOVEMENT II: The In-Between

My comfort in the chaos. My becoming in the wild.

I was forced to live in the in-between.
No one would have me anywhere else.
I learned to navigate murkiness so well, it made me unfamiliar to most—
mysterious to some, threatening to others.
Too smart. Too fast. Too much. Too quiet. Too knowing.
People called it rebellion. Cockiness. Lazy. Condescending.
But really, I just saw what others couldn't—or wouldn't.
This is where I learned to read a room without a word.
Where I first met the unseen and started listening to what lives in silence.
The in-between doesn't protect me. It doesn't love me. It doesn't harm me.
It just is.
And I exist there.

Chapter 8

What I've Carried

Pick Me
I carried the feeling that
I was never quite okay.
Not normal.
Not wanted.
Not good enough to belong to anything fully.

Somewhere early on, I absorbed the belief that I was here for other
people's benefit—
to be used, shaped, tolerated, ignored, or consumed.
I didn't know I could belong to myself.

I let people stay in my life who hurt me.
Friends who smiled
while waiting for me to fall.
Men who called pain love.
I thought that was what I deserved—
to be handled, not held.

I tried so hard to be accepted.
Rejection followed me like a shadow.
I wanted to be chosen.
Not because I couldn't stand to be alone—
but because I was tired of having to prove
I was worth staying for.

Journal Entry – 6/26/18
Whoa, here come some tears! I just want someone to love me.
Just like I am. To fight for me, my life, like I fight for the world. I
want to be someone's first thought in the morning and dreams at
night. I want someone to pray for me and imagine holding me
and playing around with me. Just me. Me and me and me. All of
me. No filters. Someone who just accepts and enjoys and seeks
me out to be in my presence. Who rearranges their life for me.
Because they want to. Because they can't get enough. I work so
hard to prove I am worthy of love. There is this huge void of
feeling unwanted. Almost discarded. Dispensable. I am enough.
Choose wisely. There is a very deep pain of not feeling wanted or
included. People don't usually come looking for me to know me
or to be my friend. I'm not interesting enough or intriguing
enough or whatever! I hate this feeling! A horrible pain. I just
want someone to choose me! Me! See me? Over here in the corner
with my hand raised. Me. Little ole me.

In the meantime...I choose me.

What They Told Me

I carried the belief that I didn't have common sense.
That something in me was fundamentally off.

I carried the belief that I was lazy—because I slept. A lot.
But it wasn't laziness.
It was restoration.
It was safety.
It was the door to the in-between.

In sleep, I could hear what others couldn't.
This was where I downloaded the messages God whispered to me.
Where my spirit recharged.
Where I processed all of the data I am constantly absorbing.
Where I started to understand that clairvoyance wasn't a curse or a

fantasy.
It was my birthright.
It was real.

Sleep was the place I became whole again—
away from the noise, away from the names,
away from the parts of the world that couldn't recognize me.

What I Gave Away

Back then, what felt normal was bending over backward to make
other people comfortable.
I was always adjusting, shrinking, apologizing, accommodating—just
to feel connected.

I shared my home with people who took from me.
Stole from me. I remember opening up gospel CD cases and finding
them empty with no CD.
Disrespected the space and still got welcomed back.
I ignored it. Sometimes I didn't even see it.
Maybe I didn't want to.

I gave away money I didn't really have.
I paid people to do things I could've done myself—just to have
someone near me.
I bought gifts, covered tabs, sent cash, made it easy.
I was generous.
So generous that somehow, I was always the one without enough.

I confused generosity with value.
And value with proximity.

I didn't have boundaries.
I had hope.
I thought if I poured enough of myself into people, they'd choose to
stay.

And the funny thing is—
no one is here.
None of the people I tried so hard for are anywhere in sight.

What I Turned Away From

Sometimes, I remember the ones who did show up.
The ones who were kind to me.
The ones who saw something real in me and tried to stay.

I think they would've loved me—
if I had known how to let them.

But I didn't know what to do with steady.
I didn't trust ease.
Their realness was so unfamiliar, it scared me off.

And so I sabotaged.
Talked myself out of softness.
Chose chaos again—
polka dots and disconnection notices.
Because struggle was what I knew.

I didn't just carry pain.
I kept reaching for it.

What Stayed the Longest

There are five things I've carried the longest:

- No one wants me.
- I'm fat.
- I am unworthy.
- I don't deserve.
- I'm unlovable.

Chapter 8: What I've Carried

They don't live in my mind every day like they used to—
but they still show up sometimes,
whispering in the tone of people I once trusted.

I didn't ask for them.
I carried them because they were handed to me early,
like hand-me-downs that didn't fit
and no one let me know I could take off.

Yet I made room for them.
I shaped my life around them.

And even now—when I know better—
I still feel them tug at me sometimes,
like a bag I thought I'd put down
and somehow picked up again.

What I Know Now

The weight is still there.
In my body. In the way people look at me.
In the assumptions they make.
In the judgment they think I can't see.

My health is critical now.
I still have time.
I still have the chance to turn it around.
And when I do, it won't just be about health.
It'll be about setting down every lie they made me carry.

Bag Lady by Erykah Badu played in the background of my mind for
years.
I never sang it out loud.
But I felt every word.
I was the punching bag.
The scapegoat.
The one thrown under the bus.

Not anymore.

I'm not a container for other people's projections.
I'm not a body built to carry what broke them.

This is the part where I start unpacking.
One lie at a time.
One belief at a time.
One bag at a time.

And this time—
I'm keeping only what's mine.

Write – 4/15/08

Write
Write about what
Write about Buff
      that he painted on me
          polka dots like gunshots on me
      that everything he said he didn't mean
Write that he hated on me
      that he declined to look past the outside of me
      that he got what he could get outta me
Write that I loved him
      gave a daughter *and* a son to him
      that I shut myself down for him
      that I never was more than his brother's whore to him

Write that I'm angry toward my dad
      that so much power my dad's had
      that I let it mix up my head
      that at times I tried to be dead
Write that I gave myself to him
      that he always made his way in

that all he wanted was to get things from me
that I didn't even matter to him

Write that my mom hurts, the worst
     that her skin wrinkles and thins
     that her life is eating her from within
     that her man is on his way out
Write that he kicked me down the stairs one day
     that he called me several times out my name
     that he got her to choose, and she refused
          to accept it

The sun will set tonight
     Right
In my living room where I am trying to write
     Write
Write that I'm beautiful, magnificent
Write that I took my soul back, I took control back
Write that my spirit released, is at peace
Write that once "I was blind but now I see"

Thank You, God, for Abriana and Diamani

-Brianna

Chapter 9

Across Borders: Colored, Free, and Fully Seen

Learning to Belong Without Blending
I've crossed borders most people don't see.
Some with passports. Others with paperwork.
Some with plane tickets. Others with permission to love children that didn't come from my body.

In 4th and 5th grade, I became fluent in Spanish through immersion school.
Before middle school, I was translating for strangers at the Cornerstone food shelf.
I didn't know it then, but I was already learning how to move between worlds—
how to listen between languages, how to belong without blending in.

Growing up our home was a host site.

A Spanish exchange student lived with us the year before I visited her in Spain. Two teachers—one from Peru, one from France—lived with us while they taught at my high school.

Later, my parents became the U.S. management team for a South African gospel singing group, and we had two different South African families live with us for months at a time. These weren't visitors. These were family. They are family.

And by the time I started traveling abroad, I already knew the difference between tourism and connection.

A World That Reflected Me
I didn't just travel to other countries.
I lived inside them.
I slept in their rhythms.
I listened before I spoke.
Ate in kitchens.
Attended schools and universities.
Went to church services and street festivals and funeral repasses.
I wasn't there to take pictures—I was there to belong.
To remember that I already did.

In South Africa, I felt something I didn't know I was missing—recognition.
Especially in Cape Town, I didn't have to explain who I was.
I felt understood—not tolerated, not interpreted, but seen.
The way people greeted me.
The way aunties offered food.
The pace. The rhythm. The music. The slang.
The food—God, the food.
There's something about the way flavor lives in that place.
It's like history cooked into joy.
In that place, I felt Colored, free, and fully seen.

Here's what I wrote after standing at Cape Point circa 1996-1997:

In an unexpected moment a crashing throb awakened my soul. My heart melted into a blood red soup as my surroundings seeped through my pores and tickled my nerves. The hair on my arms prickled with excitement as if they were dancing with joy. My eyes twinkled and my body froze all over; it was the most beautiful scene I had ever seen during my years on Earth.

A mess; a point where two bodies of water fuse; an unruly event. Underneath the surface, an intimate secret is hidden from all the world, two enemies both envious of the other's power.

In the center of a giant sparkling sapphire, a place where crinkles waft across the top of the water, a slight, minuscule chasm opened the way to a colossal explosion. The scent of the air was vile, and as the wind picked up speed and pushed everything out of its way the sky collapsed; everything was suffocated. A small amount of water rose up and sank right back down without a splash; the ocean remained still. The sky darkened and cried out loud. Once again, the water climbed up out of the ocean in a slipshod manner like a child getting out of bed. This time as it declined, the water, a bit frightened about what was soon coming, shook with humility. Then with an unhesitant burst of excitement a cascade of water exploded upward and smacked the sky's sullen appearance. This threatening alarm awakened the sky and its puffy gray eyes began to shower the earth with tears. For a moment the waters seemed to yield, giving the sky a chance to smile and glow; a ray of sunshine infiltrated the clouds and stung the surface of the water.

The Cape opened its mouth a last time and this time the enemies separated. It was not an explosion or a disgruntled burst, but a sigh of relief. Immediately everything changed. It was as if nothing had happened. A few seconds of time gone; history. No more painful perseverance. Just composure; sweet composure.

My eyes lifted and my soul fell back to sleep. My nerves no longer felt tickled and my heart was once again solid. My hairs adhered to my arms and with a turn of my back it was over.

In Spain, I learned joy
through movement.
We danced and danced
and danced all night long.
It was amazing.

Chapter 9: Across Borders: Colored, Free, and Fully Seen

Here's what I wrote at 16 (1997) reminiscing:

The city is beautiful – decorated by its old architecture; buildings stacked together neatly like pieces on a chess board. The streets are like a lab maze; no way out! Steam pours from the centered potholes in the street. The rush of the underground metro shakes your feet; old city; beautiful old city.

Morning. Tiny windows of stacked apartments open as if the building were a block of cheese and a mouse was nibbling holes into it. From these windows came clouds of wet laundry and mats, flung out the window and hung to dry. Children come, slowly at first and then much quicker, squirming like mice or even tiny ants. Shops open on the street fronts; the smell of fresh fruit fills the air. "Frescas, Manzanas, Naranjas," comes an inviting jingle; a stray warning: "¡No te toques; Tienes que comprarlos!" Animals, free to roam the streets, fiddle at your feet hoping for food or even companionship. Sophisticated adults, dressed in their very best, cramping on the street corners. Green light; everyone stampedes into the street. Buses rush by and fill the air with a dirty smell. Cars, packed tightly, their drivers honking and cursing: "¡Hay Pendejo! ¡Rápida!"

Afternoon. Shops close their fronts and children file home from school. Fire hydrants sprinkle a false rain on dancing, nude toddlers. Cars continue their hustle and bustle but in a less hurried manner. Tourists with their neck-strapped cameras waddle up and down the same streets trying to bargain with the street vendors: "Da-may esto cosa para dos dollars." Passionate giggles from the central park; lovers – kissing, boating, walking, holding hands. Loud unfriendly roars of old gypsy women trying to get your money: "¡Flores; Trenzas!" "¡Un precio barrato!"

Night. The city is lit up like a giant Christmas tree. Everyone is in the street or hanging out their balcony window. The discotheque's music is blaring, "We Are The Champions," as loyal fans parade through the streets after an overwhelming victory. Fancy ladies shaking their stuff to anyone who will give a fair price. Sixteen is the drinking age here; barrachos slumping over the benches. A cool wind invades my nose; YUK! Cigarettes! A torn piece of paper falls gently on my foot. I flip it over. M-A-D-R-I-D!

And then there was Budapest in 2010:
The slow bathhouse mornings.
The grief soaked into the city.
The way the Holocaust hovered over the streets like memory.
I can't explain it, but my body felt it.
Like something in my bones recognized the grief.
I felt most me there.
Alone but never lonely.
Soft but not small.
Free without apology.

As I stand over the river, I see the faded figures of the women and children staring into the green waters of their freedom. One-by-one they flop into the river, accompanied by the screams of the onlookers who begin to understand their fates. As I stare across the river, I see the Parliament and I feel spirits in the mist, wafting in the injustice of their history. I smell the irony stench of execution as the tears roll down my face. Passersby look on as though I am an attraction they have seen many times before.

My travel to Budapest was an extension of my history class. The semester was spent studying European history and history of Hungary. I also studied language and literature and daily culture. When I arrived in Budapest, I was amongst my classmates and teachers, none of whom I would have never thought I would be "stranded" with. Together we spent the days with a tour guide taking us to different areas of the city that were pertinent to material we had studied in our course. We were also given free time to explore the city at our leisure.

Our guide took us to the covered market where locals purchased their daily meats and breads. Here we bought items to make our own lunches and to carry snacks with us during our excursions through the city. It was obvious that we were foreigners with our broken Hungarian requests and the outrageous prices that we were charged before we negotiated them down.

Another day trip took us to Hero Square, a dedication of sorts of all previous kings of Hungary. At the time we were there, a demonstration by members of the Gypsy population was presented in the middle of the square. I saw pictures of caskets and funeral services and I could hear the lamenting of those who had lost their loved ones. I watched as the individuals present chanted protests to the rest of the citizens. It was revealed to us that the neo-Nazis had raided the Gypsy camps and opened fire; this happened less than 12 months prior to our visit.

Our visit to the House of Terror museum was scary for me. This museum represented the horrible past that Hungary experienced during Communism. Part of the tour through the museum was to walk in the dungeons that used to hold prisoners and where many people died of sickness. I could smell death and my feet could not get me out of there quickly enough. I cried when I hit the fresh air in disbelief that we as humans have a capacity to torture and mistreat each other.

Visiting the Jewish quarters and monuments brought over me a strong feeling of melancholy. To be persecuted for something you believe and a lifestyle that you choose was a difficult concept for me to understand. Thousands of people died in Budapest during the Holocaust and to stand on the same ground where they stood was a humbling and terrifying experience. I, too, would have been persecuted during such a time for being a Black person and I could not imagine the courage and bravery of the people who died in my place. Standing at the river where women and children were shot to their deaths humbled me into a thankful acceptance of my life circumstances; I remember thinking over and over, "It could always be worse!"

I spent one afternoon alone riding the metro through the city. I was not seen as a foreign visitor as many people greeted me in Hungarian and some even carried on superficial conversations with me (about the weather and such). I ended up at the bathhouse and spent an hour soaking in the natural heated pools. I witnessed individuals playing chess and others sitting close with their partners sharing a silent moment of their love for each other. I imagined that I was royalty floating around and enjoying the wealth of my free time. Here I was, thousands of miles away from my home, finding comfort and peace with myself and I was not afraid.

Another day when we were given some free time I went to the Asian market with a few of my classmates; this felt like I was in a whole different country. The language was not familiar to me and the people could tell that I was not local. When shopping in the different "boutiques" the etiquette was very different. There was little eye contact and it was much easier to get the price that I wanted. For lunch we ate at a Vietnamese food stand that prepared homemade Pho. Who would have thought that my first re-introduction with this traditional dish would be in Budapest?

From this experience I learned that I am not very different from other people in the world. My desires and goals are very similar to that of others – just accomplished in a different way and rooted in a different culture. I learned to be thankful for what I have experienced in life and I also realized that life is too precious for all the complicated and negative things that I have allowed to block my progress. I made a pact with myself to clean up the garbage that was polluting my transition to the next level of my existence.

As cliché as it sounds, my trip to Budapest was an experience of a lifetime. Leaving my two young children and traveling across the world forced me into a vulnerable (and somewhat disconnected) state-of-mind. I morphed into an invisible entity absorbing each moment as it passed, and each encounter as it happened. My senses were on high alert; I became every person that I saw, every sound that I heard, and every taste that I smelled. That moment was all that I had in the world. In that moment I realized that my existence was not my own, that it belonged to everyone before me who guided me to where I am standing in this instance.

Borders Beyond Geography

Not all of the borders I crossed came with customs lines and passport stamps.
Some came with court orders.
Some came with children.
Some came with women like Marjeana.

I was seventeen when my mother and stepdad started adopting.
First came Manny—born Chanze—at just nine months old.
His birth mother, Marjeana, was trapped in a cycle so brutal the social worker called it modern-day slavery. His father was prostituting her for drugs.

We went through the process together, as a family.
My mom. My stepdad. Me.
We went to training together and did the home study together.
I was required to pass all the background studies and fingerprint checks, too.
Also had to promise it was a safe home and my stepdad was no longer violent.

They let me name him: Immonuel. It means: have faith, God is with you.

I loved that little guy. I would go pick him up out of his crib at night and put him in bed with me. He would always fall off the end of the bed. He was my buddy. I loved him so much. I always wanted a sibling. And he was everything! He still is.

And then the phone kept ringing.
A girl.
A boy.
Another girl.
Another boy.
Each one born to birthmom.
Each one needing a home.

There was no warning.
Just a call.
Less than 24 hours to say yes.
And every time, my mother said yes.
She adopted all five.
Changed their names.
Gave them a future.
Immonuel. Alexa. Jaden. Mariana. Kai.

My Turn
When the sixth child was born—Nevaeh—my mother said no.
She had reached her limit.

And that's when I said: *What about me?*

I picked her up from the hospital at 36 hours old.
Today, she is Alyviah Grace.
My daughter.
My third.

Three years and seven months later,
I got another call.
A toddler.
Abandoned at the county hospital.

Her name was Steveana.
She had been living with her birth mother—Marjeana.

Within a week, Mikeila was home.
But she wasn't mine.

Not yet.

She was still her mother's daughter. Still her father's child. We were just the place she landed when everything else fell apart.

And that made things complicated.

Because as much as I wanted her to stay, I couldn't pray for that without feeling the weight of what it meant—for her parents to not get better. For them to lose their rights. For a system to decide that love in one house would come at the cost of letting go in another.

I didn't want to wish failure on anyone. I didn't want to root for someone else's heartbreak.
So I asked someone in my Buddhist community: How do I pray for Mikeila to be with us, without hoping her parents fail?

They told me this:
"Pray for the best possible outcome for everyone involved."

And that became my prayer.
Always.
Even today.
The best possible outcome for everyone involved.

Holding Space for Love
Through Mikeila, I met Marjeana and Stephen—Alyviah and Mikeila's not only share their birth mother, they share the same father.

The state had deemed them unfit.
Their rights were terminated.
One voluntarily. One involuntarily.
But I chose to build a relationship anyway.

Because who was I to step in between a parent and their child?

I knew what it was like to yearn—for a parent's voice, their story,
their presence. To ache with questions about where I came from and
who I came from. That longing doesn't go away just because
someone else steps in with love.

And I was in no place—*no right*—to take that from anyone.

So after Mikeila's adoption was finalized
I made it my work to hold space for all of it.
To love Mikeila and Alyviah fully and still leave room for the people
who brought them into this world.
To never require them to choose between belonging and biology.

I had to figure out how to make it work for everyone—because
that's what family means to me.
Not erasing anyone.
But expanding what's possible.

They called Stephen, Dad
and I asked her to pick the name she wanted
to be called.
May May.
That's what she chose.
That's what we call her.
All of us.

I set boundaries.
You must be sober.

You must initiate contact.
If you do that—we'll show up.

And we did.

We met them at museums.
Shared Christmas dinners at homeless shelters.
Fourth of July celebrations on Chicago and Franklin
Invited them to birthdays and graduations.
And they came. Sober. Present.
Held barbeques together in my backyard.
Let the girls wake up at their birth parents' home on Easter morning.
Even meeting aunties, uncles and cousins on both sides of their birth
families.
Let them know where they came from—fully.

When Stephen died in 2021, May May moved in with us.
She stayed for eight months.
Grieved in the safety of my walls.
Got clean.
Then turned herself in—ready to face the warrants, the past, the
system.

She still calls.
Still checks in.
Still loves her daughters in the way she can.
And I still make space for that—when it's safe.
Because healing isn't linear.
And love—real love—crosses every line we were told not to cross.

Chapter 10

The Defiant Faith

Where I Learned to Kneel
I was introduced to God through Protestant Christianity.
Specifically, the Apostolic Christian Church.

This wasn't just a belief system.
It was a lifestyle.
Like the Amish or Orthodox Jews—only modern enough to drive cars, use electricity, and have plumbing.
But not modern enough for television.
Not for movies.
Not for malls or music or dancing.

Faith in my childhood was daily and disciplined.
Every morning, I watched my grandparents kneel at the sides of their bed before they even brushed their teeth.
Then again, after they got dressed.
Then again—before and after every meal.
Then once more before bed.
Each prayer could stretch ten minutes long.
It was not rushed.
It was not optional.

We read the Bible before we ate.
After we ate.
At breakfast, lunch, and dinner.
Scripture wasn't just sacred—it was schedule.

Chapter 10: The Defiant Faith

There were two services every Sunday with lunch
sandwiched in the middle.
Ministers weren't paid. They were chosen.
They prayed over the week, then let the Bible fall open before the
sermon.
Whatever page it landed on—that was God's word for the day.

There was a process for becoming a member.
A full repentance.
You confessed every sin—not just to God, but to the elders of the
church.
Only then could you be baptized.
A full water submersion.
Only then could you marry.
And only with another member of the church.
Always without birth control.
Families were big—twelve, fifteen, seventeen children.
I have over a hundred first cousins on my mother's side.

Children were seen and not heard.
They definitely did not spare the rod.
And cleanliness *was* godliness.
Men didn't have facial hair and
White, short-sleeved, button-up shirts
with dark pants, no shorts.

Women didn't preach.
Didn't wear pants.
Didn't cut their hair.
They wore long skirts, floor-length.
Buns wrapped tightly.
Head coverings tied down like ceremony.
Longer ones for prayer.

Chapter 10: The Defiant Faith

I remember the gossip about a woman whose skirt looked like a skort.
How horrible it was said to be.

I remember watching my cousins unpin their buns at night.
Thick, ankle-length hair falling around them like a curtain.
I loved their hair.
I loved the ritual.
I loved the rhythm.

My grandfather, who was chosen to be a minister,
memorized the entire King James Bible.
I would read out loud and stumble—and he'd finish my sentence,
word for word.

There was no music in the church.
Just a pitch pipe and hymns.
No clapping.
No instruments.
No images of God or Jesus—just silence and stillness and breath.

I didn't question any of it then.
I just breathed it in like air.
Even before I had the language,
I was paying attention.

The Language of Reverence
Through my godmother's family and my immersion experience,
I fell in love with a faith that moved like music.
From alphabet songs, built altars and Pan de Muerto, to Three Kings
Day—and even a giant marimba from cans and wood that stretched
across the classroom floor.
Through weddings and rosaries. Through Spanish spoken in prayer.
Catholicism felt like poetry—ritual wrapped in rhythm.
Not because I believed every word—
but because I saw people feel something together.

I learned reverence in a Puerto Rican kitchen.
Enchiladas and pierogies.
Every single episode of *In Living Color*
on the biggest TV I could imagine.
Sade playing from the stereo, smooth and sacred.
Reverence wasn't about silence.
It was about *feeling everything at once*—
family, food, rhythm, spirit.
It was holy because it was whole.

At Blake, I attended more bar and bat mitzvahs than I can count.
Jewish classmates brought me into sanctuaries filled with Hebrew,
tradition, and light.
The ceremony. The lineage. The ancient memory.
The same God.
It felt familiar, even in difference.

At Park Avenue Church, I first realized my relationship with God was
my own.
I questioned the idea of exclusivity—
If we're all made in His image, isn't there truth in *all* of us?
I didn't believe in one way.
I believed in *what was shared across all ways*:
Love.
Dignity.
Kindness.
To help when I can.
To do no harm.
To be the best me I can be—so I can give the best to the world.

I don't know if God is male or female.
If we're made in Their image,
then God is all of it.
Male. Female.
Father. Mother.

Everything in between.

That's why I've never understood the problem with queerness.
Isn't all of it holy?
Isn't all of it divine?

Journal Entry – 1/16/17
If God is everywhere and in everything, how can you truly know
God if you limit your contact with societies, people, literature,
etc.?

Sacred Mirrors & Cosmic Maps
Jolie shakabuku'd me into Nichiren Buddhism.
She doesn't so much practice anymore.
I received my Gohonzon on New Year's Day 2014, chanting with
family.
It wasn't a rejection of Christianity—it was an expansion of it.
My pastor didn't understand.
Blocked me on social media and everything.
I believe Jesus would have
sat down in conversation and communion
with me.
I believe He would have found the love in it
and we would have connected on that mutual part.

Today I still chant *Nam-myoho-renge-kyo*.
Not to a god, but to a mirror, my Gohonzon—my highest self.
This is the practice of SGI Buddhism.
It centers you, aligns you.
Calls forth your divine, unstoppable essence.
And it's aligned with the God I believe in:
One who forgives.
Who welcomes.
Who doesn't put conditions on love.
I dedicate myself to showing up as my best self

all the time.
Every time.
I discover my limits and push myself
to fully live in my magnificence,
Or Buddhahood.
And I think that just means
shining the brightest I can shine.
Being love in a world of hate.
Light in a world of darkness.
All with the intention of
leaving a positive impact.
And loving me first.

I've also always wondered why so many Christians fear the stars.
Why they scoff at zodiac signs while quoting Genesis—

"And the Lord God formed man of the dust of the ground,
and breathed into his nostrils the breath of life;
and man became a living soul." (Genesis 2:7, KJV)

And God made the sun, the moon, and the stars
"to be for signs, and for seasons, and for days, and years." (Genesis
1:14, KJV)

That's not forbidden.
That's design.
The tide responds to the moon.
Crops yield to the season.
Time itself bends to the stars.
So why would I be any different?

I'm made of dust—
the same matter that holds galaxies together.
So of course the stars speak to me.
Of course the moon moves me.
Of course the heavens hold meaning.

I don't worship them.
I witness them.
I read them the way I read my breath—
as something alive, intentional, sacred.
The same God who formed me from dust
also marked me with a timestamp.
A blueprint.
A cosmic fingerprint.

Call it zodiac.
Call it divine alignment.
Call it intuition.
I just know this:
I am not an accident.
My timing wasn't random.
And every part of who I am was written—
in dirt, in sky, in stars.

The Color of God

I once wrote in high school:
The color of water is forgiving.
It cleanses what is dirty.
It gives life to what is dead.
It takes the shape of what it enters.
It does not panic when contained.
It breaks open when necessary.
It floods.
It crashes.
It carries.
It carves.

The color of water is the color of God.

That's the God I know now.
Not demanding. Not punishing.
Flowing. Breathing. Sacred.

But also—
capable of drowning.
Capable of crashing through the walls I thought were safe.

The God I know isn't weak.
Isn't passive.
They are vast.
Mysterious.
Able to swallow a life whole in an instant—and still, somehow, give
it back changed.

You have to learn to move with water.
To respect it.
To float, to breathe, to know when to let go and when to kick hard.

And you have to learn to move with God the same way.

Not because They are cruel.
But because They are that powerful.
That wide.
That eternal.

Reverence and fear have always lived side by side.
Even when I didn't understand the language for it,
my body already knew.

God is not where I was told to find Them.
Not in punishment.
But in presence.

In silence and in storm.

The color of water is the color of forgiveness.
The color of awe.
The color of a God who both holds and humbles.

And still, beneath the flood, I rise—
because *joy comes in the mourning.*

(literary references to both James McBride, 1996 and Maya Angelou,
1978)

Love That's Not Earned
I've loved people who left me bleeding.
People who saw my tenderness and chose to harm me anyway.
People who couldn't love me, didn't want to, or only loved the
version of me they could control.

And still... I love them.
Not in a naive way.
Not to get them back.
But because I know what it is to still be lovable—even after you've
messed up.

I've messed up, too.
Not just once. Not just when I was young.
I've broken trust. I've said things I regret.
I've been careless with hearts—including my own.

And still, I'm lovable.
Not despite those things. But alongside them.

That's hard for people to grasp.
Because we're taught that love is a transaction:
You behave, you receive. You fail, you're punished.

But that's not real love. That's control.
And the love I carry isn't a reward.
It's a recognition. A knowing. A steady flame.

When I say "you are loved," I mean:
Even if you're a mess.
Even if you've fallen short.
Even if you haven't yet forgiven yourself.
You're still worthy of love.

And that includes me.

That's what people don't understand about me.
I don't love with conditions.
I don't love because you earned it.
I love because that's who I am.

It makes people uncomfortable.
Because most love they've experienced came with strings attached.
But mine doesn't.

That doesn't mean I let people harm me without consequence.
I have boundaries.
I walk away.
I say no.

But I don't hate. I don't wish destruction.

I wish wholeness.
I wish clarity.
I wish people the same healing I'm fighting for myself.

I'm an empath. I'm clairvoyant.
I can feel when someone is carrying grief in their jaw.
When they're aching behind their smile.
When they're pushing me away because they're scared I see too much.

And usually? I *do see* too much.

I can tell when someone's angry—and where it's coming from.
I can tell when someone wants to leave but doesn't know how.
I can feel the tension before the words even form.

I've always been this way.

As a child, I felt my teachers' sorrow.
I felt spiritual presence in the room when no one else did.
I knew who had died before anyone said a name, or before the call even came.

That's how I know this:

We are all loved.

Every single one of us.
No matter what color we are.
No matter where we were born.
No matter who we love.
No matter what we believe.
No matter how we dress.
No matter what we eat.
No matter how we look.
No matter how much money we have.
No matter who or what we pray to.

We. Are. All. Loved.

Not because we're good.
Not because we're strong.
Not because we survived.

But because we *exist.*

God doesn't rank love.
God doesn't wait until you've cleaned up your mess.
God isn't moved by performance.
God already decided.

No more.
No less.
Just loved.

And that's what I believe for you, too.
Even if you don't feel it yet.
Even if no one ever showed it to you.
Even if you've hurt people and can't forgive yourself.

You are still loved.

And if you're looking for proof?
Maybe it's this page.
Maybe it's this moment.
Maybe it's the fact that I can still love you—and I don't even know you.

That's not softness. That's power.
That's how I know I'm not broken.
That's how I know *you're not either.*

Where God Meets Me Now

God shows up in unexpected places.
Not just in the pews or the prayers—
but in the mess. Oh the mess!
In the mornings when I burn the eggs and Lu tells me it will be okay.
In the car rides with my kids when someone shares something hard and everyone listens.
In the silence between two people who choose not to raise their voice.

God meets me in the moments so I don't lose myself.
When I sit on the couch with my head in my hands and no plan for what's next.
When I take a deep breath before I respond.
When I choose to rest instead of prove.
When I let myself be seen without explanation.

I used to think I had to do something to get close to God.
Pray harder. Believe better. Suffer more gracefully.
But now I know:
God isn't waiting for me to be ready.
God is already here.

Here—when my kids climb into my lap after a long day.
Here—when I set a boundary I once would've apologized for.
Here—when I cry alone in my room and say, "I don't have it today."
Here—when I wake up the next day and do it anyway.

God doesn't need a performance.
God needs presence.
And I've learned to offer that—not just to God, but to myself.

What I Wrote Before I Came Here
I believe I wrote this story.
That before I came here, I sat with God and said:
"Let me learn what I need to fulfill what I'm here to do."
And together, we shaped this life—every joy, every break.

That means I chose my parents.
I chose the pain.
I chose the beauty.
And now I get to choose how I carry it.

My children chose me, too.
That must mean I'm someone worth loving.

I'm not just biracial.
I'm half God, half human.
Made in Their image. Omnipresent. Infinite.
A storyteller with skin on.

Chapter 10: The Defiant Faith

I'm not trying to understand everything.
I know I can't—not with this body, this brain.
And I live in the in-between.
The place where nothing has to make sense for it to be true.
Where I am both here and eternal.

And if I wrote this story—
then every desire in my heart is real.
Not just possible, but *promised.*
And every experience I had (and will have)
was (and is) designed.
On purpose.
With intention.
Pre-meditated.
By me.
And so I can simply forgive.

My humanness doesn't always know how things will come to
be. But my spirit already feels it.
My energy already calls it in.
My vision already sees it.

And that is enough.

I live like it's already mine.
Because I already am who I was always meant to be.

Chapter 11

Raising While Healing

My Lifeline
They say you don't get to go back and fix your childhood.
But they don't tell you what it's like to raise your children
while your childhood is still living in your bones.

Mothering didn't wait until I was ready.
It didn't ask if I was healed or whole.

It handed me a baby—and then another—and then two more.
And whispered:

Love them better than you were loved.
Hold them closer than you were held.

And so I did.
I do.
Every single day.

What they don't say is that mothering is a mirror.
It reflects everything—your joy, your rage, your softness, your
shame.
It asks you to confront your unhealed parts...
while also packing lunches and doing bedtime stories.

My son, **Diamani**, saved me.
Not because he asked to.

But because he made life about something other than my pain.
He was the reason I got up in the morning, even when I didn't want to.
He taught me structure. Grace. Relentless, unromantic devotion.

My daughters taught me other lessons.

Abriana showed me my own strength.
Reminded me that I was worthy of softness, that love should never be earned through suffering.

Alyviah returned my laughter.
Slowed my pace.
Taught me that every moment is sacred if I'm willing to actually be in it.

Mikeila stretches my patience to its breaking point and then asks for a hug.
She teaches me how to stay in the fire without burning up.
She demands that I become new, again and again.

Each child re-mothered me in ways my own childhood couldn't reach.
Each one opened something up that I had kept sealed for safety.

Mothering Through Fire
People talk about parenting like it's about rules, routines, rewards.
But in this house—parenting is resistance.
It's reclamation.
It's the sacred act of saying:
The cycle ends with me.
I am not raising children to be compliant.
I am raising them to be free.
To ask why.
To challenge power that masquerades as truth.
To trust the fire in their belly and the softness in their heart.

To cry without shame.
To name what hurts.
To fight for what heals.

They are not here to mirror me.
They are here to mirror the world back to itself—brighter, louder,
more honest.

I mother their souls.
Their spirits.
Their scars.

I mother differently, for each of them.
I speak truth to them about their bodies, their limits, their yes and
their no.
I tell them the right names for things.
I let them play with what they like.
I let them be who they are.
I don't shape them—I study them.
And I try to love without expectation.

And still—I mother in chaos.

They have thrown chairs, broken doors, started fires, screamed
threats, wiped feces on walls.
And still—I hold them.
And love them.
Every time.

I've mothered through tantrums in grocery stores and parking lots,
ambulance rides and ER visits trying to explain that the fentanyl the
doctor is giving them for the pain will not kill them like it did their
dad, and school suspensions.
I've pulled soiled underwear from under couches, moldy banana
peels from closets, lunchboxes from beneath the furnace.
I've watched teachers misunderstand my kids.

I've watched peers turn cruel.
I've watched systems label them broken before learning their names.

And through it all—I mother.
Without a manual.
Without a promise it will get easier.
Without a roadmap for where the pain will end.

Grands, Too

People think I'm strong—and I am.
But they don't always see the guilt.
The guilt of choosing to raise two littles with FASD while my older children learned to parent themselves in some ways.

The guilt of knowing I didn't mother them all the same—and couldn't.
Of hearing my teens say they felt unloved, unseen, pushed aside.
Of knowing their stories will never match what I hoped for them.

Diamani has carried the oldest burden.
Only boy. Oldest child. Guinea pig for a mother still figuring it out.

He's struggled—with identity, friendships, grief.
With watching me show up differently for the girls.
With feeling like love had to be earned.

When he asked for a dog, I said yes without hesitation.
We drove twelve hours to get Theo—his dog, his joy.
Theo belonged to him. But he loved all of us.
Especially me.
I was his grandma. His Person.

And then—he was gone.
Run over. Killed instantly.
Taken from us during one of my daughter's unsafe moments.

I watched both of them break that day.
And I broke with them.

I mothered Theo, too.
And now I mother Mr. Jimmy and Gigi—Diamani's toy poodles, my soft-eyed grandbabies.
They teach me presence.
And that sometimes—just being near someone is enough.

The Parachute That Never Opened

I never planned to be a single parent. I never wanted to raise children without their father. I wanted what I didn't have—a family that stayed.

When Diamani was born, I believed we would raise him together. I clung to that belief with everything in me. Even as things got hard. Even as he started to pull away. I still held hope. Because I loved him. And I loved our babies. And I thought love was enough.

But being with him was like going skydiving. He got me suited up, hyped me up, made me believe this was going to be everything I dreamed. And we jumped. Together. But when it came time to pull the cord— my parachute didn't open.

I kept pulling and pulling—nothing. And I hit the ground. Hard.

But I didn't die. I survived the crash. I felt every pain, every broken bone, every cut and bruise. But he never came to visit me or see if I was okay. And then I realized: he knew I didn't have a parachute the whole time. He jumped with me anyway. Sweetest smile I've ever seen!

That kind of betrayal breaks something in you. It makes you question your instincts, your worth, your sanity.

I wasn't just heartbroken—I was disoriented. How did I end up here?

I wanted the dad I never had to show up for my kids. I wanted a family. I wanted to protect my babies from the ache of absence I knew too well.

But he wasn't ready. He was chasing someone else's idea of manhood. And I had to choose. I couldn't raise three kids—him included.

So I drew the line. And then I stepped over it. Alone.

It was the loneliest kind of courage. The kind that doesn't get praised or posted. The kind that looks like exhaustion and overdue bills and two crying babies in the middle of the night. The kind that says: I will not let this break me.

I grew up. I got strong. I healed wounds I didn't even know were open.
And I promised myself: My children will have a safe home. A place where they are free to be who God made them to be. A place where they are loved without conditions, seen without shame, and strengthened to face the world with joy. The day after Diamani's first birthday, I sat eight months pregnant with Abriana and wrote in my journal:

Journal Entry – 2/28/06
Well, my children's father...we are not married and are not together right now – things got a little tough for us so we are separated, but hopefully we are both (I know I am) working on ourselves in order to provide a solid foundation for our children in the near future.

I am actually not sure at this point if we will even be back together…the hardest part is trusting God and letting go! Whatever the outcome, I know God has a plan for me… someone is out there for me and my children (my prayer and my almost impossible hope (it feels like) is that it is their dad, obviously).

I have been so discouraged about all this—it was never in my plan, thought, desire, anything—that I would have children with a man who was not going to establish a family with me and our children. It is hard for me to come to reality with the fact that I am actually single with 2 children. I'm just having trouble forgiving myself sometimes: I should've done things in a different order. When you look back though, things wouldn't have happened any other way because I was not who I am today…

Their father, well, to best describe It, I say that he fears the world and not the Lord. He Is running around worried about what everyone else thinks and he's trying to be what he thinks a man is (he never had his dad there to teach him, or any other man for that matter), or what everyone else is telling him a man is; he is really struggling with himself. I just believe God will work it out for him whether he is with me or not.

I am confused a bit, figuring out what God's plan is for me. I want to make the right decisions because they will affect my kids, now, too. I hope to provide my kids with a safe home, one where they can explore themselves and not be ashamed about what they find.

I want them to be free to be who it is that God created them to be without judgment and ridicule. I hope to keep as much confusion away from them as possible while they develop into young adults (they should be kids as long as possible).

I hope to give them strength and teach them that they are valuable and worthy and important – that they can have, be, do anything that they want! I hope to 'protect' them while they are growing so that when crazy and confusing things DO come into their lives (this is inevitable) that they will be strong to deal with them and not succumb to vulnerability and insecurity as a result of the situation; I don't want negative situations to 'make or break' them, but to be an experience for them, something they can gain strength, knowledge and wisdom from.

My greatest fear for my children is the absence of their father. I had the hardest time without my dad, a lot of emotional problems: looking for love in all the wrong places, and dependencies and all kinds of crazy issues. I know I had a step- dad, but that was and still is a negative experience for me and I don't want my kids to have those same 'issues' that I did because no dad was there; dads are needed for a plethora of things that a mother can't give or even do for her children.

He tells me he will be back around when our daughter is born, but I have some expectations of him that need to be in order before he can come back and that makes it even more complicated... I want him there so badly, I am lonely for him but I have to put my values and those I am trying to establish for my children first; I am not going to take care of 3 kids!!! I have decided that it is better to not have him there at all than to have him in his current state; he is not stable and can't bring or offer us anything right now.

It has been hard for me to get things together on my own, but very necessary and I am grateful for the learning and growing and experience...I am definitely growing up and getting stronger!

> The emotional wounds of my childhood and early adulthood are opening up and starting to heal, and that is very emotionally draining – makes it hard to get up some mornings (thank God for my son, or I would be in bed all day long!).

The Many Mothers I've Been
I've been so many mothers.
The one who counted coins to but dinner.
Who whispered affirmations over sleeping kids.
Who bought diapers with borrowed money and borrowed hope.
The one who hoped I'd get to work on an empty tank of gas because I only had enough money in my bank account to get back home.
The one who yelled. Who regretted it.
Who prayed the kids remembered the love, not the volume.

I've been the mother who made Christmas miracles and Thanksgiving feasts.
Who Googled how to fix everything, and did.
Who cried in locked bathrooms and still showed up for bedtime.
I've mothered on faith alone.
On fumes. On fire.
And I've been the mother who slowly—quietly—started to forgive herself.

I've mothered the children I birthed.
And children I met in the middle of their storm. Children who found safety in my arms, even if they didn't call me Mama.
Even if they never stayed.

I've mothered my sisters. My friends.
My godchildren. My community.
I've mothered men who thought they needed love but were really asking to be raised.

I've also mothered the girl I used to be.
The one who didn't know she was allowed to rest.
The one who learned to smile through agony.
The one who always had the answer—but never asked for help.
I've been every kind of mother—except the perfect one.

And that's the one I never needed to be.

The Secret Rules of Life

There is a way to live that aligns with the Universe.
I've seen many people miss this step.

Whether we are Christian or atheist, Muslim or Jewish, the Universe is not a force we can escape. It's like gravity—unseen but undeniable. So no matter what you believe, or who you worship, you still have to reckon with the laws of the Universe and how they shape your life.

When these patterns began showing up in my children's lives, I started calling them *The Secret Rules of Life*. That's what I told them I was teaching them. That's what I call my blog on my website now (www.onpaperllc.com/blog). And still to this day, I remind them— they are being initiated into these secret rules for the long haul.

Here are some of the rules my children hear from me often:
1. Every day, make progress.
2. You are responsible for the delivery—not the outcome.
3. Always a beginner.
4. Everything is a choice (even your parents, even your feelings).
5. There is learning in everything.
6. We are making this up as we go along.
7. Your power is in your silence.
8. You are whole, perfect, and complete.
9. What you say is what it will be.
10. That's that. So what?! Now what?

11. It's none of your business (what people think about you or say about you).
12. Live infinite possibilities.
13. Don't touch stuff that's not yours
14. Who are you being?
15. _____ now, play later!
16. Love and be kind.
17. There are no victims.
18. Own your own shit.

Sacred Work

I'm not raising "good kids."
I'm raising honest humans.
Revolutionaries.

And I know this truth now:
I am not failing.
I am not broken.
I am not my mother's wounds nor am I my father's absence.
I am a living reclamation.
A woman being mothered by the very children I birthed.
And that is holy work.

Journal Entry – 9/30/09

I now have two children, and I've decided to parent them in a way that nurtures their self-discovery.

I outline basic morals and values for them, but I also give them space—room to build their foundations through their own experiences.

I encourage them to listen to their inner desires, and I support their achievements when those desires lead the way.

My goal isn't to shape them into something—I want them to

---

become who they already are. To grow into individuals who possess the power to shift their lives, adjust their circumstances, and define happiness for themselves.

Whether they choose to become doctors or factory workers, I will be satisfied if they've learned how to evaluate, evolve, and make new choices when needed.

This parenting style has been its own education for me.

I realized that, as a child, I was bound by my parents' internal beliefs—that any deviation from their expectations meant they had somehow failed.

I have freed myself from that.

I don't parent from fear or control. I parent from trust.

I no longer see myself as a victim—and I never truly was.
I see now that my choices shape my life.
That I get to choose again.
That I get to pursue what I desire—fully, freely.

Chapter 12

Love in the Margin

Performing For Pennies
I didn't always know I was on the edge.
Because when love is all you've ever wanted,
you'll accept whatever is handed to you and try to call it whole.

I *received* love there.
From the margin.
Sometimes it saved me.
Sometimes it broke me.

This is the story of what I accepted.
What I mistook for love.
What I kept trying to earn.

I stayed in relationships where I was never the priority—
just the fixer. The listener.
The soft place for someone else's chaos.
And I called it love.

I stayed in friendships that only existed when I was convenient—
the one they processed with,
but disappeared from when it got too real.
And I called it loyalty.

I stayed in rooms where my brilliance was borrowed but never
named.

Where I was allowed to speak, but never truly heard.
Where I was thanked but never remembered.
And I called it community.

There were years I thought love meant being available.
That to matter was to be needed.
That love lived in how well I could hold other people's
mess without ever showing mine.

But there's a cost to taking in love from the margins.
It teaches you how to make yourself small.
How to whisper your needs.
How to confuse devotion with disappearing.

It takes years—decades—to unlearn that kind of love.
To believe you don't have to audition.
To trust that love doesn't mean earning.
To know your full presence is not a problem to manage.

I'm still learning.
But I don't wait outside the door anymore.
Now, I sit at the center of my own life.

And anyone who wants to love me
will have to meet me there.
Not above me.
Not behind me.
Not when it's convenient.
With me.

Because love is something I don't have to beg for.
It's something I was born deserving.

Systems of Survival
I used to think love had to hurt a little.
That if it wasn't dramatic, it wasn't deep.

Chapter 12: Love in the Margin

If it didn't come with silence and shouting,
with slammed doors and whispered apologies—
it must not be real.

Almost every man I got involved with—
whether we called it dating or just fucking—
hurt me.
Not always with fists.
But always with something.

Yelling.
Blaming.
Gaslighting.
Silence as punishment.
Control disguised as care.
Jealousy disguised as love.

They raised their voices.
Questioned my worth.
Dismissed my boundaries.
Laughed at my dreams.
And I let them stay.

I mistook chaos for chemistry.
Mistook control for protection.
Mistook survival for love.

I let men talk to me like I was disposable.
I let them touch me like I was theirs.
I let them rage near my babies—
and still convinced myself they cared.
They loved the light I carried
and hated when it made shadows on their own mess.

I stayed, not because I didn't see it,
but because I thought I was strong enough to take it.

Strong enough to fix it.
Strong enough to make them better.

But some men don't want better.
They want a home for their harm.

I thought love was fixing.
That if I healed him enough, he'd love me back harder.
If I stayed long enough, he'd stay longer too.

And I kept being soft.
Kept bending.
Kept believing I was the problem when the house caught fire.
But I was not the fire.
I was the one holding the extinguisher—
and still apologizing for the smoke.

It took me years to stop calling pain "passion."
To stop thinking adrenaline was intimacy.
To stop twisting myself into something
that could be held without trembling.

Leaving wasn't one moment.
It was a long, quiet exhale.
A shift.
A knowing.
A reclaiming.

I didn't leave because I stopped loving.
I left because I started loving myself.

And even in leaving, I doubted myself.
Was I too sensitive?
Was I giving up too soon?
Was I broken because I couldn't make it work?

Somewhere in the silence, I met myself again.

Sampled, Not Chosen

There was one.
Not the father of my children.
But the one who stayed just close enough to matter—
and just far enough to never fully show up.
Twenty plus years.
Friends. Lovers. Ego balm.
I stroked his confidence like he was immortal.
Let him believe he was sacred.
Let myself believe that made me sacred too.

We initiated around the city—
in vans, cars, grass, conference tables, kitchen sinks.
Spontaneous. Wild. Sometimes beautiful.
And still—it wasn't love.
It was sampling.

He had other women.
Other lives.
Baby mamas. Children.
Whole stories I wasn't written into.

But I stayed.
Begged, even.
Not for money. Not for gifts.
Just for him to choose me.
Just to be *the one*.

He never did.
He told me what I wanted to hear.
Let me carry the dream so he didn't have to.

And still—I let him stay.
Because somewhere in me, I believed

that to be sampled was to be enough.
That if he kept coming back,
it must mean something.

It did mean something.
It meant I didn't yet believe I deserved more.

> ### *Journal Entry – 5/29/17*
> Once again, I have poured my love into someone who doesn't
> deserve it...How do I get so blinded by wanting someone to love
> me/accept me that I see right past the signs? He just kept me
> around to see how he could benefit. I never thought it would be
> him. I protected him for ever.

I don't tell this for shame.
I tell it because it's true.
Because love in the margin sometimes *feels* like power
when it's actually quiet permission to disappear.

And I don't disappear anymore.

Love From Other Mothers
Not all the love in the margins broke me.
Some of it saved me.

There were women who stood at the edge of my life and extended
their arms.
Auntie Marie. Auntie Ann. Annette. Pastor Yar. Diana Lovelady.
Marquita Clardy. Ms. Lena. Claire Mary.
They weren't always loud about it.
But they stayed.
They sat with me when I couldn't speak.
They let me talk for hours when I couldn't stop.
They saw me.

They told me to keep going.
They told me I mattered.
They told me I was worth more than my mistakes.

These women weren't just kind.
They were anchors.
They tethered me to a version of myself I hadn't met yet.
They loved me from the margins—but not with scarcity.
With abundance.
With commitment.
With truth.

Gracie Girl
And then there was Rachael Grace.

We met when I was in fourth grade.
She was younger than me.
Same elementary school. Same church—Park Avenue.
We locked eyes, and that was it.
We were bonded for life.

Before the world told us who we were supposed to be,
we had already decided: sisters.
Her mom told us love made us sisters.
And it did.

Then came the whispers in the hallways
about the girl with that disease.
The one with "AIDS," they said.
When I saw her name and picture
in the newspaper I called my mom:
"It's her. It's her mom."
I was devastated. I didn't want it to be her!
I cried and cried.
That didn't change a thing for me.
I loved her.

I went to her house. She came to mine.
Just never share toothbrushes and always wear helmets.
We went to appointments together, sat through medication trials,
watched new treatments steal her appetite and her energy,
but never her joy.
And she was always so silly!

She lived like she wasn't dying.
She laughed. She danced.
She jumped off bridges into lakes with me.
She sang with me. Baked with me. Grew with me.
She gave me her favorite stuffed animal to keep
so I could remember her when she did die.

We were on the Nickelodeon special together,
where she met Magic Johnson.
She called me when she miscarried.
She called me when she got pregnant again.
She called me when the grief was too heavy.
And even when she moved away,
I was the one she called when life felt like it was falling apart.

She lived knowing her life might be short.
And she made it big anyway.

When she died, a part of me laid down too.
I named Mikeila after her:
Mikeila Rachael.
Because I want my daughter to carry that kind of grace.

Chosen Bonds and Sacred Threads
They say you don't get to choose your family.
But I've spent my life doing exactly that—choosing.

I chose to stay in contact with the other mothers of my children's
siblings,

even after things ended with their father.
Not because it was easy.
But because our kids deserve each other.
They deserve siblings. Sleepovers. Photos. Laughs.
They deserve to know that just because a relationship ends
doesn't mean love has to.

We drove across state lines to keep those connections alive.
Chicago. Atlanta. Wherever they were, I showed up.
I welcomed their brothers and sisters into our home.
Fed them. Held them. Tucked them in.
Because family is not about who stays together.
It's about who shows up when it matters.

And I've always tried to show up.

Even with my own siblings—on my father's side.
Some of them didn't know what to do with me.
Some kept their distance.
But the ones who gave me a little space to belong—
I met them where they were.
New York. Alabama. Chicago. Florida. Atlanta.
I needed them to know I cared.
That I was here.
That I was trying.

I tried to hold the line together.
Tried to be the thread that doesn't break.
Tried to believe that family—by blood or bond—was worth keeping
close.

Because that's what love in the margin really is:
Making space for people the world makes easy to forget.
Refusing to let go, even when it would be simpler to disappear.
Building bridges between people who may never say thank you.

To prove we could be family, even when the world said otherwise.

Love That Holds

Love in the margin taught me something no center seat ever could.

It taught me how to hold others.
And how to let them hold me.

It taught me that love doesn't always arrive wrapped in romance or vows.
Sometimes it shows up in casseroles and phone calls.
In someone who stays on the line until the tears stop.
In someone who tells you: "You're not too much."
In someone who never asks you to shrink.

Love in the margin gave me sisters.
It gave me the mothers I didn't birth from.
The family I chose.

And now?

Now I write my own definitions.

Love is not a test.
Not a scarcity.
Not a reward.

Love is a soft place to land.
And I am building it—right here, in the middle of my life.
No longer outside the door.

Inside.
Rooted.
Worthy.
Whole.

Chapter 13

The Silence Between Stories

When Silence Was Safer
I've been loud in rooms that couldn't hear me.
And quiet in rooms that didn't deserve my silence.

I've learned to read more in a pause than in a paragraph.
To feel what wasn't spoken.
To hear the hum beneath the lie.
To trust the stillness before the answer.

That's what silence teaches you—
how to listen like survival.
How to catch the way love shifts in someone's eyes.
How to know when danger isn't loud—it's charming.
How to disappear in plain sight.

I didn't grow up telling my story.
I grew up memorizing the parts I wasn't allowed to speak.
Practicing silence like a language.
Holding back the truth until it felt like breathing under water.

And still—
there were moments I broke through.
Moments where silence didn't win.
Where I said too much, or just enough,
and felt the sting of being misunderstood.

But now?
Now I know:
Silence might have shaped me,
but it doesn't get to keep me.

I speak.
Not for shock.
Not for validation.
Because the words have waited long enough.

Not Yours to Speak
Sometimes silence screams.
And sometimes I answer back.

This piece—this roar on the page—was one of the first times I let my
rage speak without apology.
And people didn't like it.
They said I was too light-skinned to write this.
Too privileged. Too articulate. Too close to whiteness to be this mad.

What they didn't understand is that anger doesn't come with a color
chart.
That pain doesn't skip you because your skin reads "ambiguous."
That just because I wasn't always targeted doesn't mean I wasn't
always *watching*.
Carrying.
Burning.
Knowing.

I've lived with the contradictions.
Felt the stares and the slurs and the slaps.
Been called too white and too Black—in the same breath.
I've lived the legacy of both sides and been welcomed fully by
neither.

This poem is not just about anger.
It's about all the things I wasn't supposed to say.
All the history I inherited but wasn't allowed to name.
It's about the rage that builds when you're told to be grateful for the scraps of belonging you're offered.

So yes—I wrote this.
And yes—I meant every word.
Because sometimes silence isn't strength.
Sometimes, the most radical thing you can do
is scream.

I Am Angry at Black People – 2007

Historically
We are
A population that has been oppressed and mistreated;
A population that has been confused, not self-aware, with low self-esteem,
    Struggling
To find our place in society and figure out where we fit in,
Historically.

400 years
We suffered
to find a sense of safety and/or security in a society that exhibited
       and still exhibits
Alcoholic and schizophrenic tendencies of
       unpredictability, domination, and control.
We hated ourselves and passed on our trauma and self-deprecation
       generation,
           after generation,
               after generation.

With freedom we tried
       to find a place in society

Where we could walk through a department store without being followed,
or to drive without being pulled over,
>Get a good paying job,
>or do well in school without being made to believe
>>that no matter
>>how hard
>>we tried
>>we still
>Failed.
All we were left with was society's definition of
What Black is
and what Black isn't.

Society said:
>"Black is a ball player or a gangster rapper. Black is expensive cars, with tinted windows, chromed-out wheels, and loud banging music. Black is designer clothes, gold and diamond teeth, big gaudy chains and jewelry. Black is a baby daddy."
Society said:
>"Black is a drug dealer and a pimp. Black is poor. Black is a gang-banger that shoots another Black person for wearing the wrong color. Black is obnoxious. Black is a thief."
Society said:
>"Black is tight, skimpy clothes, with skin showing. Black is long colorful nails, a fake pony-tail. Black is pants belted around your hips, sagging. Black is a struggling single mother. Black is a nigger."
>>And Black people, we believe this!!

I am angry at Black people.

We continue to blame white society
>or man
for our current state,
But yet we succumb to society's definition

Of who we are
And we continue
To show them
that we are exactly
      what they told us
         we would be!

We shoot each other, we fight, we beat our women;
We don't finish school or speak proper English;
     We niggnorant
We tha dope man for our mama and our son
We tha baby mama, and not the only one
"She's not Black!"
    "I'm Blacker than him!"
      We hate
      Each Other
   "She don't struggle, look at her skin."

I am angry at Black people.

We self-medicate with
Material things
We think that's the only way to
    Be respected
        Or be accepted
           Or be worth anything.

We look a certain way, talk on a certain cell phone, and drive a
certain car
We run up bills, never pay off debts, use our children's credit.
The only option left
Is to collect the welfare check
And then the government tells us how to live.
And thus begins the cycle for our kids
    And their kids.

It's the white man
we still complain
But we are giving them the power to keep us that way.

I am angry at Black people.

Our chance in society, many thanks
Dr. Maulana Ron Karenga
       Rosa Parks,
             Marcus Garvey,
                  WEB DuBois,
                        Sidney Portier,
                              Thurgood Marshall,
                                    Sojourner Truth,
                                        Dr. King
             For your wisdom, courage, and strength

They were not drug dealers and gang bangers
with fancy cars, wearing heavy jewelry,
pants around their ankles, abandoning their families,
calling each other "Nigger..."

They refused to be someone else's definition,
        someone else's description, or
           someone else's explanation
    of who they were
and *What Black Is*, and *What Black Isn't*!

I am angry at Black people.

The First Love I Let Go
Some loves never make it into the world,
but live in you forever.
This was my first.

I was nineteen.
A college student.
Trying to hold my life together with binder clips and staples.
And then—I was pregnant.

I found out in a hospital bed, in a room meant for rest and mental healing.
There was no celebration.
Just fluorescent lights and the quiet sound of my own heart breaking.

He told me he'd leave if I kept the baby.
My parents said I couldn't live at home with a child.
That I'd have to go to a shelter.
I was terrified.
So I let their fears shape my decision.

Rachael came to see me that day.
She didn't bring advice.
She just cried with me.
Held the grief without trying to fix it.
I still feel the weight of that kindness.

Years later, I asked the father if he would have really left.
You know, if I kept the baby.
He said, "I don't know."
Really?!
That answer haunted me more than if he'd just said yes.

But none of it changes the truth:
I loved that baby.
Wholly. Fiercely. Instantly.
I loved them before I even knew what to call it.

I wrote this letter during that time.
Not because I had answers.

But because I had love.
And no place to put it.

So I placed it here—
in a letter.
In a memory.
In this book.
So they would never be forgotten.

To The Baby I Didn't Hold – 2001

I loved you since the first moment I saw you
Even though you were only 1 cm long
I loved you when I saw your little heart beating
And even when I got sick from the changes in my hormones
How beautiful you will be with pretty brown skin,
Curly hair and big brown eyes!
God planted you special deep down inside

But I need to tell you
No matter what the future may bring
I love you my first child within
I am your mommy and I'm 19 years old
I go to the local University and I am studying to be a doctor
When I met your daddy he swept me off my feet
Me and your daddy always talked about what our future would
bring
Together with children and a wedding ring.

Then mommy got sick
My emotions weren't right
So off to the hospital for four days and three nights!
I learned of your existence on my second day in
And my heart fell in pieces with lots of confusion
I was carrying a child inside of my womb and
Now I'm in school...what do I do?

My first reaction was to birth you into this world
And to raise you to be a strapping boy or girl
But my heart brings me tears
When I think of the pain
That I went through when I grew up...

What could I possibly offer to you?
I'm single, I'm young and I'm trying to go to school
You would have a daddy that would definitely be there
But I'd be the one giving most of your care
For you I want the best things that this universe could bring
So I'm left with this decision
Bring you in
Or send you back to heaven!

I still haven't made up my mind
But it hurts me to have to decide
If I give birth to you on September 19
Will I be able to give you the things that you need?
Will I be able to provide you with finances and things?
Emotional support, that's the hardest thing
I want to so bad
Hear you cry the first time
And hold you in my arms
And rock you goodnight
But in the end is it fair for me to bring you here
Will you get everything that you deserve?
That is my biggest fear!

The other option is to send you above
With a wonderful lady
Who will give you much love!
She will hold you tightly until I come one day
She will never let you down
And you will have everything that you need!
But whatever decision I make remember one thing

I love you and that's why a decision has to be made.

It won't be based on what others say and think
This is between you and me and God
No one else; no other thing
No matter what choice that I make
Every September 19 I will celebrate
For you have life and you are living inside of me
I'll celebrate all the things you are, were and could ever be!
My baby
No matter what I must do
My decision is 100% focused on you!

Please forgive me if I ever let you down
I will try my hardest so you will never frown
With prayers and with thought
A decision will be made
I don't know if it will be tomorrow
Next week
Or the following day
But I loved you from the first day that we met
Any you I will never forget!

My life will always be touched by your little heart
Whether you will be here on earth
Or in heaven if we part
I just want to do what is right for you
Mommy loves you...I really do!!

Life on Park: Disappearing in Plain Sight

There are stories you only tell when the danger is over.
Life on Park was one of them.

It was 2003, the year I turned 22 years old. I was living in a two-bedroom apartment on Park Avenue in South Minneapolis. From the outside, it looked like freedom—my name on the lease, my own mailbox, my own fridge. But it wasn't freedom. Not really.

That apartment belonged to the streets.
To the chaos.
To the men who came and went.
To the noise.
To the numbness.

I paid rent.
I cleaned obsessively.
But I was just borrowing the space—trying to survive it.

There were weeks I didn't know who was sleeping on my couch.
Days when food ran out and nights when the weed didn't.
We smoked. We danced. We played Spades until dawn.
We made meals, braided hair, stored guns.
It felt like something—almost like community.

But it wasn't safe.
And it wasn't love.

I let myself become the background music to other people's lives.
I took in their stories so I didn't have to feel my own.
I let the apartment become a revolving door of people trying to escape something.
Including me.

When my friend got pregnant and moved out, it all got quiet.
And the quiet felt suffocating.
So I went searching for noise.
Found it in the arms of another friend, and then another.
We partied. We traveled. We found ourselves backstage, front row, in strangers' hotel rooms, in trunks riding up to 30 miles.
We were reckless, wild, unheld.
And I mistook all of it for freedom.

Chapter 13: The Silence Between Stories

Then I met the older brother of the neighbor across the street.
The one who watched me while I scrubbed my floors on my hands and knees.
He needed fixing. I needed distraction.
I let him move in.
I bought him clothes. Cooked his meals.
Took some blows from his frustrated fists.
And called it love.

He introduced me to ecstasy, alcohol, and a kind of risk I hadn't known before.
We got into cars with weapons I didn't ask about.
We smoked with men whose names I didn't remember.
We ran the streets like our lives didn't matter.

I wrote a piece years later about my 22nd birthday.

That night, we pulled up to a corner house—a block from my apartment.
We were supposed to light a blunt in memory of someone who'd just been killed.
But someone tipped off the cops.
And suddenly the car was surrounded.
Guns drawn. Red and blue everywhere.
I couldn't hear anything, but I saw everything.
His lips moving. My hands shaking.
"We have these guns," he whispered.

That night, I was arrested.
For the first time in my life.
My birthday ended in handcuffs,
in fear,
in the back of a squad car.
No calls.

No plan.

I spent the night in jail.
Cold, concrete quiet.
The next afternoon, Rachael came to pick me up.
He stayed an extra day.
And when he got out,
he was back at my place like nothing had happened.

A few months later—
he locked me in a closet after throwing me to the floor
and sexually assaulting me.
He turned up the music. Pulled down the blinds.
I cried until my throat was raw.
I thought he might kill me.

When I called the police, I didn't do it because I was ready to leave.
I did it because I didn't know what else to do.
My landlord told me I had to move.
Let me stay until I found a new place.
That's when I left Life on Park.

Happy Birthday to Me 2003– 2/4/08

Dressed like midnight
I disappear
My homegirl doesn't feel right
So we took her home.
Sticky, syrupy, crepes and cream
Her whispers his hidden dreams
RIP Juan – let's blow one
But wait, we'll get some leaves.
He's smiling at me – I am beautiful!
I feel his eyes tasting me.
Is that police in front of my windshield?
Am I on TV?

"We've got these guns, Bree."
Really?! We?!

Life on Park wasn't just a place.
It was a season of vanishing.
Of surviving without living.
Of performing strength while secretly unraveling.

No one knew.
No one asked.
And I wouldn't have told them even if they did.

I kept smiling.
Kept saying yes.
Kept letting dangerous people define my value.
Kept pretending that being needed was the same thing as being loved.

But I was never really seen.
Not then.
Not by them.
Not by me.

And when I left, I didn't look back.
But the silence followed me.

I didn't speak of that time for years.
Not because I forgot—
But because the words didn't exist yet.

Now they do.
And so I speak.

Movement II Summary: *The In-Between*

This is where I stopped pretending.
Where I stopped trying to be chosen.
Where I let go of the boxes and built something softer.
I found pieces of myself in hard conversations, in quiet rage, in sacred solitude.
I grieved the versions of me I had to outgrow.
I told the truth, even when it shook my voice.
I didn't find peace here—but I found presence.
And in presence, I found power.

I didn't arrive at clarity with ease.
I stumbled into it—
Bruised faith, scraped hands, and a pen still learning how to tell the truth.
The in-between didn't break me.
But it stripped everything that wasn't mine.
And in that raw, terrifying emptiness—
I started to listen to the voice I'd been burying all along.
It was mine.
And she had something to say.

MOVEMENT III: What I've Claimed

What I choose. Who I be. Where I start.

I no longer apologize for how I see the world—or how I move through it.
I don't shrink, soften, or shape-shift to fit someone else's idea of who I should be.
I get to live free. I get to live full. I get to live mine.
I'm the same when no one's watching and when everyone is.
That unsettles people—the rawness and the polish, together.
I've made peace with how I got here.
I'm not bitter. Some places still ache, but I don't explain them anymore.
I just am.
I'm not beginning again.
I'm beginning for the first time.
I'm writing toward a life that's calm, kind, safe, vibrant.
A life full of travel, learning, laughter, growth, and wonder.
This is the part where I start living.
Because finally, I am the author of what's next.
And from here—my real life begins.

Chapter 14

Undoing

The Invitation
Where would I be without Claire Mary?

I didn't seek her out. She chose me. Handpicked me. Out of my chaos. Out of the version of myself that didn't yet know she was worth loving. She pointed, and said, "You. I'm going to coach you." Just like that. No room for debate. No pretense.

And she had conditions: Pay her. Bring her a large, sugar-free vanilla latte with sugar-free hazelnut, and skim milk. Call her each week. Call on time. Fill out the prep form. In advance.

I didn't know what to make of her at first—this tough-as-nails white lady from New York with a mouth like a sailor and a spirit like a sanctuary. But there was something in the way she saw me.

She wasn't gentle about it. She didn't whisper her care. She just showed up. Firm. Fierce. Unapologetic. And the thing with Claire

Mary is this: I never felt like I had to earn her love. She chose me. And held on ever since.

And I didn't know how much I needed that until it was already happening.

Learning to Show Up
Claire Mary didn't just coach me—she taught me how to arrive.
How to be present.
How to be responsible to myself.

Every week, I was expected to call her on time. To submit a prep form. To come prepared to the conversation.

The first time I didn't fill out the form, the shame I carried was overwhelming. Not because she shamed me—but because I had never been held accountable like that without being punished or abandoned.

It took years—years—for me to learn how to be late and still call. How to say, "I didn't finish it," and not ghost. How to name where I was and stay in the relationship anyway.

That was Claire Mary's gift.
She didn't let me avoid myself.

She knew that accountability wasn't about perfection—it was about presence. About telling the truth. About not hiding when you didn't have it all together.
She showed me that showing up, even in mess, is enough.

Redefining Responsibility
Claire Mary told me: "You are the author of your story."

It didn't land as a cliché. It landed as permission.
It meant I didn't have to keep living from old scripts.

I started to understand that self-accountability was love in action. That being responsible for my thoughts, feelings, and choices didn't mean blaming myself—it meant reclaiming my power.

She taught me that I decide what I let in and what I release. That I am allowed to feel, and also choose how I respond. That boundaries aren't punishment—they're invitations.

And that means other people are responsible for themselves.

She taught me how to stop being other people's scapegoat. How to stop adjusting myself so others wouldn't be uncomfortable. How to recognize that if drama kept showing up in my life, it wasn't just bad luck—it was because of who I was being, and what I was allowing.

And if I could shift who I was being? My life would shift too. Like magic.

And not the dark kind. The holy kind. The kind of magic that lives in surrender and alignment and truth.

The Undoing
Undoing what?

The idea that I had to earn love by giving myself away.

Claire Mary made me write a contract with myself: *I am a confident, whole, accepted, beautiful woman.*

And I repeated it—again and again and again—until the words stopped sounding like lies.

She helped me unlearn martyrdom. The belief that I had to suffer to matter. That I had to make other people's lives great so I could feel worthy.

I learned that "no" is a complete sentence.
That I don't have to explain my choices.
That I don't have to accept what doesn't honor me.
And if I ask for a loan,
It is not their business what for.

Undoing is rarely easy, but it is simple.

It's the moment you recognize the belief you've been carrying doesn't belong to you—and you put it down.

I stopped expecting people to meet me where they had never learned to go. And I let that be okay.

I stopped carrying inherited stories about struggle, suffering, silence.
I let go of over-performing, over-explaining, over-accommodating.

I let go of "should."

And that made room for so much more.

Notes From The Beginning
My life was messy.
But something sacred was happening.
After coaching with Claire Mary, I wrote down after one of our earliest sessions.
I didn't know it then,
but this was the moment the undoing began.

What We Discussed – 11/25/07
(Coaching Notes, lightly edited for clarity)

Chapter 14: Undoing

- Brianna being okay with Brianna
- Stop giving up on myself and punishing myself
- Stop "shoulding" all over myself
- Be grateful for my kids
- A man will come when I don't need one—rather when I want one
- Read my contract to myself all the time and post it around my house
- Turn myself over to the Universe and trust the Universe
- A man won't come until I'm okay with me
- I get to stop giving in to my seasonal cycling, instead of just accepting—wow, it's another season
- Stop trying to control it. Just let it fall.
- Trust the Universe. If I know I'm right, it doesn't matter.
- I know how my boss works, and I chose to continue to work for her
- I'm having a breakdown—and it will enhance my breakthrough
- Build a thicker skin (by saying my contract)
- Write a letter to my parents and step-parent. Don't blame. Don't be a victim.
- I get to make my own family
- I get to meet people with completely different lifestyles
- Know: it will come (my family)
- I start with negative comments. I get to be positive and move out of the negative
- Getting over being a victim starts with my language
- My self-image will not change until I'm okay with myself
- I give up on myself
- I need coaching. There is no more canceling
- Coach is disappointed that I fell back so far (I am too)
- I get to work on myself 24/7. My contract is the last thing I say before bed
- I get to move on
- I get to stop giving my boss so much power. Her humanness shows every day

• I missed reporting my wins and achievements—I get to start next time

What I Learned
(Reflections written at the time, followed by present-day notes)

I found it interesting to be told that I am punishing myself. I did not look at it that way before. And that is what I had been doing to myself. Wow!

That was the first time I saw the pattern. The first time someone called it by its name. I wasn't just hurting. I was hurting myself.

I learned that I get to coach every week and not miss any sessions. I fell back and was disappointed about it.

This is where I first recognized my own patterns of avoidance. Where I first felt the sting of disappointing myself—and decided to keep showing up anyway.

I get to focus on my contract say it to myself all day long. I get to put it up all over my house. The more I say it I will start to believe it. I will build a thicker skin in the process.

That contract saved me. I didn't believe it at first. But I said it anyway. Over and over again. And eventually, the words made a home in me.

I get to trust the Universe and give up control. If I know I am right and doing the right things, then I do not have to worry about anything.

This is when surrender stopped sounding like weakness. When I first felt the power in letting go.

I get to stop giving people so much power. We all shit the same way!

Listen. If you know, you know. That was my first lesson in leveling the playing field. No one gets to be God in my life but God.

I get to stop "shoulding" on myself.

And I did. Eventually. Not all at once. But this? This was the start of freedom.

And now?
Now I understand this list was more than a recap.
It was a roadmap.
Each bullet was a brick in the foundation of who I was being—
not by adding more, but by taking off everything that wasn't mine.
This was the moment I started to trust
my voice.
To choose my path.
To come home to myself.
This was the beginning.

The Return
Years before I ever knew I'd be a coach, Claire Mary
saw something in me before I saw it in myself.
She planted seeds that bloomed slowly—but surely.
She was grooming me for a life of
happiness, joy.
Showing me how to share it with others.
And she never gave up on me.

She's still here.
Still calling me forward.
Still refusing to let me disappear.

I hear her voice whispering in my mind.
That's that. So what?! Now what?

That's Claire Mary.
That's her in my bones, in my work, in my presence.

And now, I'm a coach too.
I walk with people the way she walked with me.
I hold space.
I ask hard questions.
I name what I see.

I know now—I didn't just learn how to heal.
I learned how to lead.

Journal Entry – 5/30/17
The biggest lesson I've/I'm learned/learning is that nothing is ever as it seems. The ones who were good for me, I pushed away in discomfort, and the ones who were no good for me, I held onto with dear life. The lesson is about me. It's always been about me: what I'm worth, what I deserve, my confidence, sticking up for myself, how I've let others treat me. And who I am being in the midst of all of this. I've held on way too long to people that were never meant to stay. And I build my life and my identity around pleasing them and their happiness. I've neglected myself and my children, so busy worrying about other people. And so I grow. And I've learned not everyone is going to like me all the time, or my choices, and the best decisions are absolutely the hardest ones. I've learned not to second-guess myself, and to do what I think is best at all costs. I've learned that how I intend to come across to others is not always how it is perceived or received, and to be a leader, I get to be humble and open to new learning. I've learned that I don't need anyone but myself, and I am good enough – good enough as I am. I am embarking on a new journey and it is challenging – but it is not more than I can handle and I am better for it. I don't have to prove anything to anyone! I am exactly where I'm supposed to be right now at this time.

Permission to Stop
Undoing was not just about letting go. It was about building differently. It was about permission. To stop performing. To stop managing people's feelings. To stop proving. To start choosing.

Undoing didn't break me. It made me soft where I was once armored. Fierce where I was once afraid.

It made space for sovereignty.
For clarity.
For calm.
And most of all—for choice.

Because now I know:
I am not my past.
I am not my pain.

I am the author.

And this chapter?

This one is mine.

Chapter 15

I Am Brianna

My Name, My Knowing
Before the world told me who I had to be,
I was Brianna.
Pure. Joyful. Flirtatious.
The girl with a quick wit and a wide heart.
Friendly in every room, funny without trying,
attractive in that way that made people wonder where I came from.
Generous without needing to be asked.

I was love.
Not the idea of it—the actual thing.
Kindness wrapped in curiosity.
A beginner, always. Open to the lesson.
Unbothered by not knowing, because I trusted I would learn.
That's still true.

Journal Entry – 11/26/22
What is my story...what is holding me back? Where is "joy?" It's all about me. Everything, every experience, every person, it's all about me. How do I get unstuck? Fuck is taking so long?! What is it about me? The world the way I see. The way I see me. I am conditioned. I am offspring of a society built on white supremacy ideals, that's the DNA in me, in you, in us all. I see I can't be me. How do I fit into this box they made for me?

I am Brianna.
Not the Brianna you make up when I walk in the room.
Not the one you whisper about.
Not the one you think you see but don't.

I am the Brianna who carries truth in her bones.
The one whose name meant strength long before she knew she'd
need it.
The name my mother gave me when she didn't yet know how hard
the road would be.
The name that carries regeneration—like a phoenix, not just
surviving, but rebirthing.
The name that carries fear, too, because I have always walked into
the unknown
and still chosen to stay.

The Energy I Bring

People feel me before they hear me.
My energy enters first—reverent, still,
like Spirit walking through the door.
I am powerful. I am mysterious.
People gravitate toward me because I do not flinch when I see them.
I see the rawness. I hold the ache.
I listen with more than my ears.
That kind of seeing makes people uncomfortable.
Especially when they are hiding from themselves.
I move through cultures, languages, and systems—fluidly.
That ease unsettles people. Makes them suspicious.
They call it two-faced.
But really, I'm just fluent—
in contradiction,
in code,
in the in-between.

I see what they can't.
And they hate that I say it out loud.

They've called me sneaky.
They've accused me of things that never lived in my hands.
I used to wonder why.
Was it projection? Was it fear?
But I don't wonder anymore.
I just know who I am.
I am sacred.

The Versions I've Been

I've lived many versions of myself—
daughter, student, outsider, peacemaker, protector.
Single mother. Multiple times.
Coach. Partner. Sister. CEO of my own becoming.

I've held every role a sibling can hold.
Raised as an only child.
Became the oldest when my mom started
adopting my five younger siblings when I was 17.
The youngest among my dad's kids—until my younger brother came
around later when I was already 18.
Now, technically, I'm the middle child.

And I've held nearly every role inside an organization:
Board member. Board training consultant.
Financial donor. Volunteer.
Executive Director. C-suite leader.
Director. Manager. Supervisor.
Trainer. Consultant.
Staff.
And yes—recipient of services.
And yes—all of the paperwork and the invasion of privacy and
dignity.

I've led in programs.
I've led in finance.

I've led in fundraising.
I've led in operations and administration.
Not as a visitor—but from within.

I've worked across sectors—
education, health care, housing, re-entry, justice, prevention.
I've walked the halls of schools and universities,
shelters and hospitals,
prisons and policy meetings,
outreach centers and corporate offices.
I've stood inside food shelves and board rooms,
domestic violence shelters and real estate closings.
I've processed federal financial aid,
answered hotlines, waited tables,
cashiered at the grocery store, cleaned toilets,
recorded television and radio PSAs
and built coaching frameworks for people no one else knew how to
reach.

So when I talk about systems,
I'm not theorizing.
I'm remembering.
I'm reporting back.
And I'm refusing to pretend I don't know what I know.

But none of those labels erased the root of me.
I am Brianna.
And I don't shrink anymore. Not for my mama.
Not for anyone who wishes I would fit more easily
into the outlines they drew for me.
I don't soften my edges just to be held.

If you want me in your life,
you must choose me.
I no longer audition.

My Purpose Is to See

My purpose is to see.
That's it.
I was sent here to notice what others overlook.
To find the quiet places in people—the parts that want to be seen
but never know how to ask.
I see so they know they matter.
I see so they know they're real.
And to never let someone feel invisible in my presence.
That is my ministry.

Living in alignment with that purpose means
being open to everything.
Judging no one.
Believing God is in all of it,
even the messy parts.
Especially the messy parts.
Being willing to sit down and learn
from the most unexpected people and places.
And to model that humility—on purpose.

Boundaries, Fierce Love, and Soft Edges

I've raised my children like prayers.
Loved people on purpose.
Whispered life into the forgotten.
I've chosen peace over proving,
presence over performance.

My boundaries are different now.
They aren't about how much I can take.
They're about how much I'm willing to give.
And that giving—
that's reserved for the ones who see me back.
No more invisibility.
No more being the unchosen one.
If you want my energy, you must honor it.

I am fiercely protective.
Of my babies.
Of the dignity of people.
Of kindness, even when it's hard.
I'm not soft in the way the world expects.
I'm soft in the way a river shapes rock.

At home, with my kids' laughter echoing in the kitchen,
leftovers on the stove, hair piled high, sink full of dishes,
that's where I laugh loudest and cry softest.
That's where the truest Brianna breathes.

Journal Entry – 1/13/20
What do I contribute to my family? I contribute my whole self. I
contribute my time and attention. I contribute kindness and
helpfulness. I contribute money and other resources. I am a
foundation and a role model. I contribute my knowledge and my
truth. I contribute my present-ness. I contribute love. I contribute
strength. I contribute ideas. I contribute options and new ways of
doing things.

I Am the Prayer
I hope when people think of me,
they feel encouraged.
Cheered for.
Believed in.
Seen!

I hope they remember I was kind.
And that I showed up the same in every space—
whole, flawed, sacred, true.

That's what I want the world to remember.
That I gave it my all.

That I was present.
That I loved like it mattered

I'm not learning who I am anymore.
I'm living it.

My legacy is simple and wild:
We are all worthy.
We are all love.
We are all here for a reason.
God lives in every face.
Kindness is never wasted.
And we're making this up as we go.

There are no rules but the ones that feel good to your spirit.
That feeling of "yes"—that is where the Creator meets you.

This is not fluff.
This is not fantasy.
This is divine.
This is real.

And I am Brianna.

I carry my name like a prayer.

The Walking Contradiction
To love myself
as a biracial Black and white woman
is to commit treason against the programming.
It is to love and accept the very parts of me
this world raised me to hate.

To say:
I see the kink in my hair—
the curve in my body—

the fire in my voice—
the softness in my spirit—
and I love them.
I claim them.
Even though I was taught to question them.
To fix them.
To *choose* sides.

How does that work, y'all?
How do I reconcile the way my shame was nurtured
and now be expected to perform healing?

You want my wholeness
without naming your harm.
You want my peace
without acknowledging the war you raised me in.

I am loving the parts of me
you called too loud.
Too much.
Too ghetto.
Too white.
Too anything-but-holy.

You taught me to reject the pieces of me
that didn't fit your narrative.
And I believed you—until I didn't.

But I know now:
Every piece of me is holy.
Every curve, every curl, every contradiction—
designed.

The hair you tried to tame.
The body you tried to shrink.
The voice you tried to silence.
The questions you said were disrespectful.

The dreams you laughed at.
The softness you mistook for weakness.
The fire you tried to extinguish before it grew into something you couldn't control.

All of it.

And I love her.
Not in spite of,
But in defiance of the silence I was left in.

Chapter 16

Abundance, Infinence & Beyond

The Law of Infinence
Abundance means overflow.
More than enough.
Extra.

If you ask, you will receive.
But somehow, "abundance" got put on a shelf.
It started to feel reserved.
Like there was only enough for some,
and the rest of us had to wait our turn.

Even the word abundance started to feel like it had a cap.
But that's not what God gave me.
That's not what lives in my spirit.

What lives in me is *infinence*.

Infinence is infinite abundance.
It has no end.
No cap.
No gatekeeper.
No approval process.
No secret code.
No "when you've earned It."
No "when you're ready."
It just *is*—the moment you say it is.

When you declare,
when you decide,
it is so.

That's the law. That's the truth.

This journal entry was a turning point. I didn't know it yet, but I was about to unlock something deeper than hope—I was about to remember my birthright. Infinence isn't just light at the end. It's the power to *be* the light. To move, even before you understand.

> ### *Journal Entry – 6/26/18*
> There's got to be a light at the end of all this, the beginning of the next. When and how is my weight loss going to happen? Why is it such a hurdle? Fuck! I am not happy with how my body looks or feels...I've hesitated to put my pen to paper. Why do I not want healing? Why don't I believe in myself? Why do I want to fail? What is this darkness holding me back? Do I need an answer to move on, or do I just simply move on?

We're Making It All Up
Infinence doesn't belong to the few.
It's for anyone.
Anyone willing to claim it.
To live in it.
To receive it.
To give it.

Whatever you make it to be is what it will be.
We forget that the things we believe in—
organizations, families, neighborhoods—
they are only real because we show up
and act as if they're real.
We each play our parts, which we cast ourselves

and the scenes unfold right in front of our eyes.

We are making this all up,
and that's the most miraculous part.

The Process of Receiving
If it's meant to be, it will be.
There is nothing—*nothing*—that can get in the way of infinence.
But to receive it, you have to go through the process.
You have to be open.
You have to know you're worthy.
You have to behave like it's already yours—
not entitled, but entrusted.

You have to *give*, too.
Genuinely.
Without manipulation or transaction.
Give because that's who you are.
Give because you already have enough to pour.

We Could Walk on Water
People say, *trust your gut.*
That's real.
It's the instinct that knows before your fear speaks.
It's the quiet voice before doubt creeps in.

Like a multiple-choice test—
don't go back and change the answer.
You knew the truth the first time.

That's the sin, really.
The missing of the mark.
Not because we're evil—
because we doubt.

That's why we don't walk on water.
Not because we can't.
Because we *doubt*.

But if we didn't—
if we knew our own magnificence
and lived in it with our whole chest,
we would walk on water, too.
We would fly.
We would bend time.
We would love without armor.

Journal Entry – 1/16/17
I get to have a life. My own life—free from anything or anyone
else. More than a life. I get to live. I get to be present. I get to be
right here, right in this moment. I smell the air. I hear. I feel the
temperature; I absorb the energy. This moment is me and I am
this moment. It's time, Bree. Jump. You can fly! And if you still
doubt and fall, I'll catch you. Jump. Until you soar. Like an eagle.
Fly!

What's Meant for You
Anything can come to you.
Anything is yours.
And more than likely—
the very things you desire
were placed there *because* they are meant for you.

So get up.
Make it so.

You already have everything you need
to have everything you dream.
That's not fantasy.
That's God.

That's infinence.
And it's mine.
And it's yours.
And it's now.

The House That Was Already Mine

In July 2008, I reached out to the bank
to refinance my car.
I thought I was being responsible—
making moves, getting my money right.
But I didn't know I was setting something sacred in motion.
A month later in August, my banker finally called me back.
Delayed by a family emergency.
Still, she got it done.

And that same month—a house was built.

I didn't dream about homeownership right away.
In October, a friend—a single mother like me— told me
She was buying her own home.
And I felt something stir.
So I asked. And then I called.
I filled out the application.
Took the class.
Got my credit report.
Wrote the letters.
Started the work.

I didn't just move on paper.
I moved in spirit.

I visualized.
I drove by the house I wanted.
Imagined the Christmas tree in the living room.

The key in my hand.
The joy in my bones.

By February 2009, I had paid off all my collections debt.
And with a 587 credit score, I was approved for a mortgage.
By April, I moved in.
A brand new home.
Built the same month the banker called me back.

Before we moved in, I hired a Feng Shui consultant.
She walked through the space, did a blessing, then looked at the numbers:
9996
She asked, "Did you choose this house on purpose?"
"No," I said.
She smiled. "The number 9 is powerful. Sacred. Lucky. I thought you knew."

I didn't.

Scrap Paper Promise
Seven years later, I almost lost it.
You know the story:
I was a single mother, exhausted, stretched thin,
doing everything I could.
But it wasn't enough.
I got behind.
Not by choice—by circumstance.
And I reached that place where I could afford one monthly payment—
but they won't take it unless you pay everything.
So I kept getting more and more behind.
And everything felt impossible.

I was using the food shelf.
Answering the same intake questions every time:

What's your income? Are you behind on bills? What else do you need?

That day, I mentioned my mortgage.
Told the volunteer I was struggling to get assistance approved.
She asked me what bank.
"US Bank," I said.
She paused.
"I used to work there. I retired from US Bank."
And then:
"Richard Davis is the CEO. He's a good man. Very kind. He's based right here in Minneapolis."

She wrote his name on a piece of paper.
I tucked it in my wallet and forgot about it.

Until months later.
September 16, 2016.
A mortgage representative told me flatly,
"There's nothing else we can do. You'll need to contact an attorney."
And then she hung up.

I crumbled.
Cried hard.
Diamani and Abriana came into the room.
I told them I was sorry.
That I had failed.

Diamani—clairvoyant, like me—asked,
"You lost the house?"
I nodded.
But even then, I wasn't done.
Something told me to go into my wallet
And I started digging.

And that piece of paper fell out.
Richard Davis. CEO. US Bank.
I searched his name, looked up the bank's email format, guessed his address:
richard.davis@usbank.com.

And I wrote him.
Poured out my story.
Asked for mercy.

It was 3:00 p.m. on a Friday.

That weekend, I cleaned my house.
Moved like it was still mine.
Because it was.

Email to US Bank CEO – 9/16/16
Mr. Davis –

My name is Brianna Miller and I am a mortgage customer with US Bank. My account number is...

I have been in default on my mortgage payments since March 2014. For various reasons my income began to slowly decrease up to March 2014, and then completely stopped in September 2014. And I have not been able to make any payments because I have never had the full balance owed to pay all at once.

I have 4 children, two biological and two adopted; I am a single mother. My two youngest have special needs from Fetal Alcohol Spectrum Disorders and other cognitive, development and social/behavioral diagnoses. Although I have been seeking work for the past two years, the demands of my household have many times held me back from securing full-time employment.

I have been working with the Loss Mitigation Department since June 2014, and there has not ever been a resolution reached for my situation. I recently submitted an application "Request for Mortgage Assistance."

I called today and wanted to know the status of my application, and I was told that it was too late and they can't stop the sale date of my home! What?! I was told that I could send in the application and have a facially complete package five (5) [days before the scheduled sale date] then the sale date could be postponed. I find out today that it cannot and now I am going to be without a home.

I know you do not know me, and you do not owe me anything, but I am asking for mercy today. Please, please help me!!

Sincerely,
Brianna Miller

Delivery Confirmed
On Monday morning, the phone rang.

"Brianna Miller?"
"Yes."
"This is the complaints department at US Bank."
Oh, what did I do now?
She continued: "A complaint was filed on your behalf from the executive offices.
We're stopping your sheriff's sale. We'll be investigating."

Within weeks, I was approved for mortgage assistance.

I never met Richard Davis.
But he became my angel.
Because infinence doesn't just give you the dream—
it gives you the courage to fight for it again.

And there's more:
Last year, I pulled out my birth certificate.
Top right corner. State file number.
The last four digits?
9996

You can't make that up.
I thought the miracle was the house.
But the miracle was the remembering.
The returning.
To who I am.
To what is mine.
To what was always waiting
the moment I said yes.

Chapter 17

Walking With People

Holding Space
I don't lead from the front.
I don't push from behind.
I walk beside people.
In the middle of their journey. In the middle of mine.
No hierarchy. No fixing. No performance.
Just presence.

When we walk side by side,
neither of us is in charge.
Sometimes we trade steps.
Sometimes we take turns leading.
But mostly—we just go.
Together.

What people don't always understand
is that the space I hold doesn't belong to me.
It isn't mine to fill.
It's mine to protect.
To dominate only in service of the one who needs it.
To make sure the light stays on for the person in the center of it all—
the mother, the leader, the child, the story, the soul.

I don't hold space to be seen.
I hold space so *they* can be.

I've walked with people through everything.
At the edge of death after chemo didn't work.
Through the quiet grief of a stillborn birth
and the miraculous scream of a newborn's first breath.
Through addiction. Through loss.
Through the heartbreak of having to let go.
Through wedding ceremonies and funeral programs.

I've walked with strangers—like the mother at the shelter
who handed me her choking baby without hesitation.
Because she could feel it—
that I was *with her.*
That I would carry her fear until her baby could breathe again.

This is what walking means to me.
I don't show up with answers wrapped in bows.
I show up with breath.
With stillness.
With questions most people are too afraid to ask.
Not because I need the answers—
because I know they already hold them.

I carry mirrors, not just maps.

Differently The Same
And always—
I see myself in them.
In all of them.
When I coach.
When I mother.
When I speak.
When I serve.

There is always a part of me showing up, too.
I see the part of them that doesn't want to break the cycle,
but doesn't know how to stop it either.

The part that still hopes, even when hope feels like a scam.
The part that wants to be held without being fixed.
I see the version of me who stayed too long.
Who left too early.
Who tried to do both.
I see the me who made decisions from fear.
The me who loved from lack.
The me who said yes just to feel chosen.

That's how I've learned to lead with grace.
Not from a place of knowing better—
but from knowing the ache.
I've walked out of courtrooms with women
who remind me of the girl I used to be.
I've sat across from leaders who perform confidence
while quietly asking if they're enough.

That's how I've learned to set judgment down.
Not because I've outgrown the struggle,
but because I remember it.
All of it.

We are all fighting for the same things out here—
just differently the same.

Defining the Walk
Walking is not just metaphor.
It's movement. Direction. Design.
It's the map we wrote before we arrived here—
etched in our spirit, before our body knew the path.

Your walk is yours.
Mine is mine.
No two are the same.
And they were never meant to be.

Chapter 17: Walking With People

That's why judgment doesn't fit.
Because how can I judge a story I was never asked to live?
How can I assess your direction
when your soul's GPS was never synced to mine?

The walk is sacred.
Even when it looks messy.
Even when it scares people.
Even when it pauses at corners others avoid.
Even when it begs for breath, or money, or mercy.

I've seen people reduce someone's entire humanity
to a cardboard sign on a freeway exit.
"I feel bad for them," they say.
Or worse—
"Do you think they're really homeless, or just on drugs?"

And I think—
What does it matter?

Their walk is not a spectacle for your judgment.
Their request is not your invitation to dissect their worth.
You get to decide: Yes or no.
Give or keep driving.
But you don't get to shame the walk.

Lately, I've been reminded of this over and over—
People handing me feedback I never asked for,
suggestions packaged as concern,
truths wrapped in superiority.

I ask for a night's shelter,
and I get a sermon.
I name a need,
and I receive a list of how I should be better by now.

Chapter 17: Walking With People

And I wonder—
since when did asking for help
mean I had failed?

I will not shrink the purpose of my walk
to satisfy someone else's discomfort.
I will not stop asking
just because people mistake humility for weakness.

A closed mouth doesn't get fed, right?
And I refuse to starve
just to appear strong.

You can say no.
That's your walk.
But don't shame mine
for daring to ask.

We are each walking
an intentional, divine design.
And the more we remember that,
the less we'll need to explain ourselves
to people who were never meant to understand us.

This doesn't mean we stop caring.
This doesn't mean we strip ourselves of empathy.
But real empathy isn't feeling sorry for people.
It's understanding that we're *all* out here trying to make it.
Trying to love and live and stay soft in a world that demands
hardness.
Trying to make choices that align with the *truth inside* us.

Empathy means knowing we're all walking—
just differently the same.

Chapter 17: Walking With People

It means we stop interrupting other people's path
with our projections, our judgments, our need to be right.
It means we only insert ourselves
when we can actually help—
and when help is *wanted*.
When we've been invited in,
not when we've barged through.

Knowing yourself deeply
doesn't mean you'll never need help.
It doesn't mean you won't fall.
It doesn't mean your walk won't include detours,
pauses, breakdowns, or deep valleys.

Sometimes the help is *part of the design*.
Or the refusal to help, a sign.
Sometimes the breakdown *is the bridge*.
It doesn't have to look pretty or be status quo
To be the way it's supposed to go.

You can be powerful *and* ask for help.
You can be self-aware *and* still not have all the pieces.
You can be walking in your purpose
and still need to sit down and breathe.

Walking With Myself
Most recently, I've had to learn to walk with myself.
And I didn't do it willingly.
So the universe and God shook everything up
until I had no choice but to walk alone.

I learned to be with myself—
not just *by* myself.
To sit in stillness without running.
To cry without needing a witness.
To laugh and mean it.

To talk to God out loud
and feel the echo in my own chest.

I kept showing up for the girl inside me—
the one who used to beg to be seen.
I made her tea. I asked her questions.
I stopped judging her tears.
I stopped abandoning her at night.
I chose her every day.

That's what it means to walk with myself.
Not fixing. Not rushing. Not hiding.
Just being here.
On purpose.
With me.

Some days, I walk slow.
Other days, I sprint.
There was a day I felt it—
a sudden, undeniable knowing.
That I had walked myself through hell
and hadn't even realized how far I'd come.

I didn't just survive.
I stayed with me.
In the panic. In the silence.
When no one else checked in, I did.

That day, I stood still
and saw myself fully.
I didn't need permission.
I didn't need applause.
I just knew.
I am it.

Journal Entry – 4/23/13
I get to show up for me! I get to believe in me! I am worthy. I am deserving. I can do me, love me, prosper me, grow me, be me, be free. I'm me.

I am my greatest obstacle. Me.
I am my greatest hero. Me.

My life is whatever I want it to be… in my wildest dreams.
I can be an Indian princess. I can be rustic and live on the range; I can live in Europe; I can own a house; I can win the race!
And whatever I choose, those are mine. I do them all. I can succeed.

It's really me. I am it. I am the hero. It's me.
I am raising children. I have graduated. I am successful in my career. I am healthy.

I will do whatever I want to do!

The Gift of Walking
And here's the thing:
No one is really unseen.
That's the myth.
People aren't invisible.
We just stop seeing.
Or we refuse to look.

And we must do better.
Every day.
To offer platforms, spaces,
presence—
so each person can reach the fullness of their God-given magnificence.

I don't walk to fix.
I walk to witness.
To reflect.
To remember.

And if we keep walking long enough—
side by side, breath by breath—
you might just remember
you were never lost.

We Are Not God
Here's what I know for sure:
You do not know more about another person
than they know about themselves.
Periodt.

It is not possible.
You are not their spirit.
You are not their Creator.
So when you claim to know what's best for someone else,
when you say "I'm just trying to help"
but your help comes wrapped in assumption or expectation,
you are not helping.
You are *harming*.

It is selfish.
It is cruel.
It is ego dressed up as concern.

But worse—
is when you believe you know them
better than they know themselves.
When you assume they're confused,
or lost,

or unaware of their own truth
just because their path doesn't look like yours,
or it doesn't make sense to you.

That is not love.
That is erasure.
That is spiritual arrogance.

We were not assigned as stewards of each other's purpose.
We don't get to rewrite the design.
We don't get to correct what we don't understand.

If you truly want to love someone,
witness their walk with reverence.
Support when invited.
Offer when asked.
And even when you don't agree—
trust that they know something you don't.

That's what it means to honor the walk.

When the Walk Ends
Some walks aren't meant to last forever.
Some people were never meant to reach the end with you.

I've had to learn when to stop.
When to step away.
When presence turns into pain,
and witnessing becomes wounding.

I've had to unlearn the lie that love always means staying.
That loyalty always means silence.
That helping means holding on.

Sometimes, walking with people means
knowing when to bless the road
and let them continue without you.

I've ended journeys
not out of anger,
but out of wisdom.

I've let people go—
and mourned,
and exhaled,
and been grateful for what was.

And when I've looked back,
I've realized:
even the walks that ended
made me more whole.

Chapter 18

A Love Letter to the In-Between

The First Time I Slipped
Remember?
I was three.
It was in the basement of a church.
It was a daycare.
It still is now.
It was nap time.
A blue mesh cot. Stackable. Small.
I was supposed to be sleeping.
I was supposed to be safe.
But I wasn't.
My body was being touched in ways it shouldn't have been.
And something in me said: *Go.*
Not with my legs.
Not with my hands.
Not with a scream.
Just *go.*
So I did.
Not out loud.
Not with movement.
But inward—so deep and quiet no one could follow.
Everything slowed.
The air thickened.
Sound dropped away.
Colors dissolved into gray.

I wasn't floating.
I wasn't dreaming.
I was *somewhere else*.
I could still hear. Still see. Still know.

And in that moment, I found something no one gave me—
a place of my own.
I didn't know what to call it.
But I kept returning.
And over time, it became the safest place I had.

The Disappearing That Kept Me Alive
I slipped again.
And again.

When someone slammed a door too hard.
When kids at school laughed too long and I wasn't sure if it was about me.
When I got called "fast" before I understood what it meant.
When I got told I was too Black here, too white there.
When the girls at school smiled in my face and whispered behind my back.
When I learned to disappear before I ever learned to fight back.

I became fluent in slipping.
Sometimes it was survival.
Sometimes it was strategy.
But it worked.
Every time I slipped.
It became instinct.
Like blinking.
Like breathing.

The in-between became a place I could go without asking for permission.
A place I didn't have to earn.

A place where I didn't have to explain why my face looked sad when my mouth said I was fine.

It's where I made sense.
Where my contradictions didn't need translation.
Where I could be all of me—quiet, loud, brilliant, raw, angry, soft, lost, found.

The Call That Took Me There and Back

On the one-year anniversary of my grandmother's death, I dreamt of her for the first time.

Journal Entry – 2/13/98

I fell asleep at 6 p.m.
It must've been a long journey.

The phone rang. In the dream—and in real life.
Because I answered it. I said, "Hello?"
A voice said: "Branna? It's Grandma."
I asked her where she was.
She said, "I'm dead."

And suddenly I was there—wherever *there* was.

A room with computers. A table. A screen. My grandfather, smiling.
My grandmother was there, too, working, putting files into folders, recording something I couldn't understand.
I asked if I could stay.
She said no.
"You have to go back. But you will come back.
Not for a very long time."

I remember crying. She cried too.
I asked, "There's not supposed to be pain here, why are you crying?"
She said, "I'm not sad. I'm happy to see you."

I woke up at 7 a.m.
I had been gone for 13 hours.
The phone was off the hook.

When I Started Going There On Purpose
Eventually, I stopped slipping by accident.
I started going on purpose.
When a room felt off.
When someone smiled but their spirit said otherwise.
When I needed to remember who I was without all the noise.

I stopped trying to explain myself in real time.
I stopped chasing clarity in spaces that didn't want to understand me.
Instead, I paused.
Went inward.
Found my breath.
Listened to the silence behind people's words.

The in-between became my reset button.
My altar.
My escape and my return.
It was where I went to find myself
after the world had tried to scatter me.

What the World Tried to Take
The world kept rewarding people who picked a side.
Who chose certainty.
Who made themselves small and smooth and clean.

I didn't.

I held too many truths.
I couldn't play along.

So I got called arrogant.
Or confused.
Or intimidating.
Or condescending.
Or dramatic.

But what I really was—
was awake.

And contradiction made more sense to me than congruence ever did.
Because the in-between taught me how to hold more than one truth
at a time.

That's not confusion.
That's capacity.

How the Hurt Became Help
I used to treat the grief like it was a parasite.
Feeding off my joy.
Feeding off my worth.
But I sat with it.
And it fed me instead.
The shame became clarity.
The rage became discernment.
The silence became presence.

And the parts I was told to fix—
my knowing,
my sensitivity,
my vision,
my contradiction—
they became my power.

In the in-between, I got to be all of it.

What the In-Between Gave Me

Chapter 18: A Love Letter to the In-Between

I used to think the in-between meant something was wrong with me.
That I didn't belong because I was too complicated.

Too Black.
Too white.
Too sensitive.
Too smart.
Too uncontainable.
You know my story now.

I thought the in-between was a punishment—
a glitch in my story that I needed to fix or hide or outgrow.

But now I know:
it was the gift.
It was the only place that didn't ask me to perform.
Didn't ask me to choose a side.
Didn't ask me to explain what I already knew in my bones.

It's where I stopped shrinking.
It's where I stopped translating.
It's where I stopped trying to be the version of myself that made
other people feel comfortable.

In the in-between, I remembered how to just *be*.

It gave me back my breath.
My intuition.
My sharpness.
My softness.
My sense of time.
My body.
My voice.

It didn't rescue me.
It raised me.
And it showed me that I was never broken.

And the greatest thing it gave me?
I no longer have to explain who the fuck I am.
Not here. Not now. Not ever.

That's what freedom feels like.
That's what clarity feels like.

That's what coming home to yourself—fully, unapologetically, and without a single need for permission—feels like.

Love Letter to the Reader
If you've lived in the in-between—
not just visited it, but *learned its landscape*—
you already know what I mean.

You know what it is to hold your tongue when people praise your clarity
but flinch when it turns to truth.
You know what it is to walk into rooms that weren't built for you
and still find a way to *be there without being erased*.
You know what it is to see through people
before they even know what they're showing.

You're not broken.
You're not lost.
You're not too much or not enough.
You're fluent in a language they haven't learned yet.

And if you're just arriving—if you're new to the in-between—
let me say this gently:
This space will not hold your hand.
It won't perform for you.

But if you stay long enough,
it will show you things you've spent your whole life trying to name.

There's no map.
No rules.
But I'm here.
And you're here.
And that's enough.

Love Letter to the In-Between
You didn't come softly.
You came through basements and bruises.
You came when the world wouldn't hold me.
You came when I needed to disappear.

You held every version of me
until I was strong enough to come back and hold myself.

You didn't ask me to make sense.
You didn't ask me to choose.
You didn't ask me to be easy.
You just asked me to be real.

And now I return to you not in hiding,
but in reverence.

I don't back down.
I don't explain.
I don't negotiate.
I come as I am.
I stay as I am.

And I will leave when I'm ready.

I don't fear the dark anymore.

Chapter 19

The Possibility of Me

What is A Possibility?
I used to think "greater than anything you can imagine" meant
someday.
Now I know it means here.

It means *me*.

And I almost missed it.

This book is mine. This voice, this clarity, this craft—mine.
I didn't chase it. I *became it*—without even realizing.
And now the sky that used to scare me?
Feels like home.

I was always a writer.
But I didn't know it would look like *this*.
I didn't know I was writing my way into the kind of freedom that
can't be measured.
This is greater than anything I even knew to ask for.

And then, I remembered
when Bettie Spruill said,
"A possibility is something that isn't,"
I felt the words tattoo themselves inside me.
I scrambled to write them down—
not because I didn't understand them,

but because I did.
Immediately.
Entirely.

That's what I am.
I wasn't.
And now—I am.
The fact that I exist at all is nothing short of miraculous.

Becoming the Artist
For years, I lived in a cyclone of mistruth.
That I had to be a certain way.
Fit a certain mold.
Speak, think, love, grieve, lead, or show up
according to someone else's rules.

But the heavens opened
when I threw all of that away
and decided to be.
To be me.
To be whatever I wanted.
To take the next step—sometimes blindly—
and trust that the ground would rise to meet me.

And it always did.
Everything around me now is because of who I am being.
What I choose.
How I think.
What I believe.
And all of that—all of it—is mine to define.

That's what possibility means.
It means freedom. Liberation.
It means I get to make something out of nothing.
And I did.
I made me.

By every statistic,
I shouldn't be here.
Shouldn't be thriving.
Shouldn't be whole.
Shouldn't have four beautiful children.
Shouldn't be sane, let alone powerful.

But I am.
I survived.
And more than that—
I stayed.

Even when I didn't want to.
Even when no one chose me.
Even when I was told over and over again—explicitly or silently—
that I was not enough.
I chose me anyway.

Someone Believed
Uncle Mike thought I might be something.
Lissa Jones did too.
Maybe they didn't know what it was exactly,
but they knew—
that when I got ahold of it,
it would be big.

And they were right.
Because now I see it clearly:
There were forces fighting me every step of the way.
Trying to silence me.
Break me.
Bury me.

And I kept going
for one reason:

I was still breathing.
So I couldn't die.

I realized I had a place in this world
the moment I saw how my children looked at me—
like I was theirs.
Like I mattered.
Like my presence was enough.

For God to take a chance on me
means I am worthy.
It means I am protected.
It means I am loved.
It means God trusted me—
trusted my free will—
to become exactly who I was designed to be.

And I honor that trust
by getting up each day.
By being kind.
By bestowing permission on others to become their own
possibility—
even though they've already had it all along.

A Prayer and A Possibility

The times I've doubted my possibility the most
were not when strangers didn't believe in me—
but when my people didn't.
When the ones I loved, protected, and gave everything to
couldn't choose me back.

That's a pain I still carry.
But it hasn't stopped me.
Because possibility is not given to you.
You claim it.

You live it.
Even when no one else sees it yet.

Diamani's prayer as a child still echoes in me:
"Thank you, God, for making me come true."
And two decades later, Bettie gave language to it.
To "come true" is not about becoming worthy.
It's about becoming real.

Following what your heart says—
even when the world throws shade.
Even when it costs everything.
Even when no one claps.

Radiant Resistance
My life is a living act of resistance
because I name the invisible injustices
and take the hits when I do.

I speak the unspoken.
I sit with the unseen.
And when the bullets come—
I heal.
I rise.
And I come back, again.

My life is radiant
because every time I rise from the ashes,
something new is born.

I used to think my life was something to survive.
But now I know—
it is something to create.

Every day I wake up,
I make the impossible possible.

Every time I say yes to myself,
I bring something into being.

I am not a composite of broken pieces.
I am not a mistake.
I am not for everyone.
But I am for me.

Because I am the possibility.
The possibility of *me*.

This Is Me

This is the chapter where I stop explaining myself.
Where I stop asking for permission to be full, to be fierce, to be
whole.
Where I say: this is me—no modifiers, no disclaimers.
I don't just tell stories.
I make meaning.
I write toward liberation.
I live in infinence.

And I get to name the next chapter of my life.

It took me decades to see myself clearly—not as what others needed
me to be, but as what I always was: a writer. A builder. A truth-teller.
A seer. A daughter of the wind and the page.
This book, this body of work, is evidence of that.
I wrote a memoir, yes. And I also wrote a movement.
One that breaks silence with song. One that bends genre and
expectation.
One that says: You don't have to fit their forms. *You are the form.*

I didn't set out to with any outcome in mind.
But *The Possibility of Me* became a text so alive, so layered, it
demanded to be studied.
It teaches healing through craft. Wholeness through structure.

Belonging through language.
It is creative nonfiction. It is poetic resistance. It is sacred instruction.
And it came from me. From a girl they called too much, too smart, too knowing.
Now, I call her enough.
More than enough.
Infinite.

The more I read my own words, the more I see what I was trying to say all along.
That I come from the in-between.
That I carry contradictions on purpose.
That I will never be soft in the ways they want, and that softness is not required to be good.

I don't need their canon.
I am my own.

I wrote this to be *real*.
To be free.
To leave a map for others who are wandering in the fog, looking for themselves in the pages.

I am not beginning again.
I'm beginning for the first time.
And from here—my real life begins.

---

free to be... – 2013

O beautiful
For spacious skies
For amber waves of grain
For purple mountains
Majesty
Above the fruited plains

America, America
God shed his grace on thee
And crown thy good
With brotherhood
From sea to
Shining sea

Discriminate
Intimidate
Inequality
Bureaucracy
It seems like I spend my life
Fighting for the right
To live a life
That pleases me
Frees me
From the chains
That keep me
But yet
Little opportunity
Given me
Am I really free
To be me?

Assimilate
Hide my face
Be like people who are white
Don't speak what's truth
Keep secrets
To protect
My dignity
Free me from their
Insecurities
Of the beautiful blackness
Of Me
Why?

For my whole life
Do I fight
For the right
To be half black
And half white
And gain flight
Into new heights
But still I rise
And you seem surprised
That I find strength
In the lies
And refuse to stay behind
I will continue to fight
Even if I fight
My whole life

You listen to my story
Now
Because I stand
In your face
Any other time
You see me
Differently
Because of my
Face's race
Where will you be
When they try
To hold me back?
Or can you not see that?
Where will you be at?
While I continue to fight
Will your privilege keep you
Oblivious
And never allow you to see
Or distinguish
That we are not actually different

But a product
Of a similar
Existence
Yet I will never receive
Your same
Privileges

Will you read the statistics
And see
That I am not in it
Will you give me an opportunity
Or will you blame it
On my lack
Of experience
Am I not an American
Like you?
Do I not deserve my 40 acres
And my mule?
Or is it because
You are afraid
To see the beauty
Continually growing
In me
You must recognize
The power
In my brown eyes
So you put on a disguise
To hide
Your true intention
Of holding me in confined
Dimensions
Or do you see it
As an intervention
To sober the blackness
Of my reflection

Chapter 19: The Possibility of Me

Continue to make promises
That are pretend
Just to keep me content
Is it that you see my potential
As detrimental
To your experience
Or do you see an image
Of me
In yourself
And you can't help
But be ashamed
That my existence
Might have been different
If you had allowed me
To keep
My last name
The same
Will I get a chance to develop
My magnificence
Or does it frighten you
That I am aware
Of my
Ontological resilience
Would it please you
If I sit down
Right this minute
And keep my emotional
Black experience
For my African-descended
Brothers and sisters
Will these words even make
A difference
Or does it feel to you
As a transgression
Into your
Existence

Chapter 19: The Possibility of Me

Home of the brave
And land of the free
America,
Set me free to be
Set me free
To be
Me

I'm me
I'm me
And that's all I can be
I'm me
I'm me
Here's my vulnerability
I'm free
And you can't stop me
I'm free
And that's all I can be
(—Willow Smith, "I Am Me" 2012)

Is me.

Movement III Summary: *What I've Claimed*

This is not a story of fixing.
It's a story of reclaiming.
Of turning toward myself and saying, *yes, you.*
I walk with softness now—not because I'm weak,
but because I'm finally strong enough not to armor up.
I trust my no. I follow my joy. I speak my name with reverence.
There are still questions, still stretching, still grief.

But I belong to me now.
And that's the most radical thing I've ever done.

Epilogue: Written Into Being

So yes, I made it here.
From the Land of Isn'ts.
From the space between breath and body,
between before and becoming.

I made it through the pages I hadn't yet written.
Through the silences I didn't think I could survive.
Through the storms that didn't name me
and the stillness that finally did.

I remember now:
I didn't come here to perform.
I came here to *be*.

Not to fit the mold, but to melt it.
Not to follow the path, but to speak it into existence.
I am not the girl wondering if she belongs.
I am the woman who knows she does.
Who doesn't need permission to be seen.
Who *is* the light, even when no one is looking.

I am the one who came from a place without edges
to build a life with no ceiling.
Who walks with her own shadow and still chooses the sun.
Who stopped asking, *"Am I allowed?"*
and started answering, *"I am already here."*

Because the truth is—
the Land of Isn'ts was never empty.
It was waiting.
For someone bold enough to believe.
For someone brave enough to begin.

For someone broken enough to need it
and whole enough to claim it.

That someone was me.
And maybe... that someone is you, too.

So if you made it here—
if you made it all the way through the unspoken, the undoing, the unknown—
then welcome.

You don't have to become anyone else.
You don't have to go looking.
You are already the story.
You are already the answer.
You are already the possibility.

Now write the rest.

With love and fire,
Brianna

The Possibility of You

You made it. Through my story. Through your own.

This is not a workbook.
This is a doorway.
There's no right way to enter. No wrong way to feel.
This space is here for you—to linger, to question, to remember, to write, to rest.

You are invited to explore what this story stirred in you.
You are allowed to say what hasn't been said before.
You are safe to begin again—on your terms.

Let this be a beginning—not a conclusion.
You are the author now.

Begin Here
Let yourself land.
Take a breath.

Place your hand on your chest and ask: *What did I feel while reading? What am I still feeling now?*

Write that.
Just that.

Reflections from What Made Me
You don't need to have the answers.
You just need to be honest.

- What stories were handed to you before you could speak?

- What parts of your early life still live in your body?

- When did you first learn to shrink?

- Who did you have to become in order to be safe?

- What pain have you been carrying so long, it feels like part of you?

You are allowed to set it down now.

Reflections from The In-Between
This is where the shape-shifting ends.
This is where your voice begins.

- What version of yourself are you outgrowing?

- What truth are you finally ready to name?

- Where do you still disappear—and what would it take to stay?

- What spaces have held you in silence?

- What would it mean to live in the murky middle without apology?

You don't have to be clear to be whole.

You just have to show up.

Reflections from What I've Claimed
This is not a story of fixing.
This is a story of returning.
Of remembering.
Of rising.

- What do you know for sure now?

- What does it look like to live your life on purpose?

- What boundaries are you ready to honor?

- What power are you no longer willing to give away?

- What is the possibility of *you*?

You are already a declaration.
Speak your name with reverence.

Creative Invitations
These are not tasks. They are portals.

- Write a letter to the version of yourself that kept going.

- Describe your own "Land of Isn'ts." What lives there? What doesn't?

- Imagine your story as a map or a song. What does it sound like? Where does it go?

- Fill in the blanks:

I am no longer

_____.

I am learning to

_____.

I am claiming

_____.

Closing Blessing

You don't have to make sense to be sacred.
You don't have to be fixed to be whole.
You don't have to be chosen to belong.

You are already a possibility.
And you are already here.

The Way I Speak the World

Some people inherit rules. I inherited questions. I created language. I made meaning out of what wasn't—and wrote a way of being into the world.

These are the codes I carry.

Some are whispered. Some are declarations.

Some are names I gave to what I've lived.

Some are the secret truths that shaped me.

Part One: The Language I Live By

Passing

Not a compliment. Not a reward.

"Passing" is what they call it when your appearance gives you proximity to whiteness, safety, or privilege.

But to me, it has always felt like erasure. A way people tried to explain me away.

I never asked to pass. I asked to be seen.

Passing is a condition put on you by others. It's a survival mask—one I didn't choose, and one I've spent a lifetime peeling off.

Biriyani

Not home, exactly—at least not in the geographic sense.

Biriyani reminds me of South Africa. Of family. Of a place where I didn't have to explain being Colored—because it was already a thing.

It's warm. Spiced. Rich with memory.

It's what comfort feels like when you're seen without explanation.

It tastes like culture without translation.

Revolutionary

Not loud. Not always.

Revolutionary is being kind when the world tells you to be cruel.

Revolutionary is choosing to rest in a system that demands your

exhaustion.
It's raising kids with love and not fear.
It's showing up as yourself—fully, freely, without waiting for permission.
Revolution is not a moment. It's a way of being.
And sometimes it looks like saying "no more" and meaning it.

The In-Between
My home. My refuge. My lens.
It's not limbo—it's liberation.
The space where you're not quite this or that.
Too Black. Not Black enough. Too loud. Too soft. Too much of everything and not enough of what they wanted.
But in the in-between, I see clearest. It's where I meet myself. Where I hear God.
Where I know things that haven't been spoken yet.
You don't find the in-between—you access it.
And once you do, it never lets you go.

Disobedient Faith
The kind of faith that doesn't sit quietly in a pew.
It questions. It wrestles. It flips the tables and still believes.
Disobedient faith is what rises when the church fails you but God still speaks.
It's the sacred yes in your chest even when the rules say no.
It's unchurched, unmuzzled, unafraid.
It's not about pleasing—it's about presence.
And it's the most honest kind of belief I know.

Caucasity
The audacity of whiteness—unchecked, entitled, and loud in its wrongness.
Caucasity shows up like it belongs everywhere.
It questions your expertise.
It centers itself in your grief.
It cries when held accountable.

It's the boldness of being wrong *and* in charge.
Joel Martinez named it in 2012, but I've been surviving it my whole life.

Niggnorant / Niggnorance
A word I created. A survival lens.
Niggnorant is when internalized oppression puts on a show—loud, unbothered, and convinced it's right.
It's when harmful thinking gets passed off as culture.
When refusal to grow gets framed as loyalty.
When hurt people mock healing, and pride themselves on staying the same.
It's parroting the language of white supremacy in a Black tone.
It's resistance to change, dressed up as realness.

Chosen
Not just selected.
Chosen is felt.
It's not about being picked first.
It's about being seen—fully—and embraced as is.
Chosen means someone didn't walk away when they could have.
Chosen is what I've always wanted to be.
And what I now require.

Differently the Same
My shorthand for humanity.
We do things in our own ways—sing, cook, worship, parent, grieve.
But underneath it all, we want the same things:
To be seen. To be safe. To be loved.
We are more alike than we are separate.
We're just differently the same.

Possibility
Something that isn't... yet.
But could be.
Possibility is the moment before creation.

It's the breath before the yes.
It's me—before the world told me who I had to be.
Possibility is what I live for.
It's the miracle of saying yes to what hasn't been—yet.
The decision to rise, again and again, and make it so.

Infinence

Not just abundance—infinence is abundance without limit.
It is overflow with no ceiling.
Where abundance ends, infinence begins.
No approval process. No "when you've earned it." No gatekeeping.
Just truth. Just is.
Infinence belongs to all who declare it.
It's the knowing that you already have everything you need to have everything you dream.
It's not for the few. It's for anyone.
And it changes everything.

The Law of Infinence

The spiritual law that governs how infinence flows.
It states: what you declare becomes.
No waiting, no proving, no gatekeeping.
The moment you say yes, it's set in motion.
It's not about earning—it's about aligning.
You already have what you need to receive what you want.
That's the law.
That's infinence.

Part Two: I Said What I Said

These are the truths I've learned, lived, taught, and spoken into being.
They are not laws.
They are not mantras.

They are codes—
quiet and deep and unshakable.

The Secret Rules of Life
1. **Every day, make progress.**
   It doesn't have to be huge. Just forward. Just faithful. Just one step.
2. **You are responsible for the delivery—not the outcome.**
   Say it. Show up. Let go. The result isn't yours to carry.
3. **Always a beginner.**
   Stay teachable. Stay tender. Expertise is a myth—presence is the truth.
4. **Everything is a choice (even your parents, even your feelings).**
   This one stings. But it sets you free. Choose again.
5. **There is learning in everything.**
   Especially the mess. Especially the pause.
6. **We are making this up as we go along.**
   No one really knows. Start over. Make it up. Make it yours.
7. **Your power is in your silence.**
   Stillness speaks. Keep something just for you.
8. **You are whole, perfect, and complete.**
   Even when healing. Even when hurting. Nothing missing. Nothing broken.
9. **What you say is what it will be.**
   Your words are alive. Speak wisely. Speak truth.
10. **That's that. So what?! Now what?**
    Don't get stuck in the story. Shift. Move. Begin again.
11. **It's none of your business.**
    What people think about you. What they say about you. Not. Your. Business.
12. **Live infinite possibilities.**
    Refuse smallness. Refuse scarcity. Let your life stretch past what's been seen.
13. **Don't touch stuff that's not yours.**
    Energetically. Emotionally. Spiritually. Physically. Hands off.
14. **Who are you being?**
    Not what are you doing. Who are you *being* while you do it?

15. **_____ now, play later!**

     You know the blank. Sometimes it's work. Sometimes it's cry. Sometimes it's wash the dishes. Fill it in. *Then* go play.

16. **Love and be kind.**

     It's that simple. And that radical.

17. **There are no victims.**

     There is pain. There is injustice. But you are not powerless. Your story is still yours.

18. **Own your own shit.**

     Name it. Hold it. Don't hand it off. Responsibility is power. And power is freedom.

Chronology of Included Writings

This memoir isn't made of chapters alone. It's stitched together from pieces of writing I carried with me across decades—journal entries, poems, class assignments, memories written in real time. Some were scrawled in notebooks. Some typed in grief. Some were never meant to be shared.

I chose them—out of hundreds—because they speak to the parts of me that lived quietly between the louder moments. I did not arrange them chronologically, and that's intentional. This book was never meant to follow a timeline. Healing doesn't happen in order. Neither does remembering.

What follows is a list of the writings included, named in the order they appear in the book.

Chronology of Included Writings

1. *Journal Entry* – October 30, 2026, 7:03 PM
2. *Grandma of Mine* – circa 1997
3. *Things About Me I Would Change* – September 25, 1997
4. *The Other Side* – Spring 1999, 12th grade
5. *Facebook Post about George Floyd* – May 20, 2020
6. *The Building I Live in Was Knocked Over* – January 14, 2008
7. *Coke* – circa 1996–1997, 10th grade
8. *Poetry Collection (Friends, Him, Untitleds, Robin Red-Breast, The Sunset, Seasons, etc.)* – circa 1994–1995, 8th grade
9. *Mommy Told Me* – circa 1995, 8th grade
10. *My Mother's Rose* – circa 2000, age 19
11. *Journal Entry – My Mom is Magnificent* – January 15, 2020
12. *Essay – Today I Met My Mother* – March 22, 2013
13. *Journal Entry – Being Chosen* – June 26, 2018
14. *Spoken Word – Write* – April 15, 2008
15. *Madrid (Narrative)* – circa 1997, age 16
16. *Cape Point (Narrative)* – circa 1996–1997
17. *Budapest (Narrative)* – April 2010

Afterthought: I Can't Keep My Mouth Shut

There are some things I held back—out of protection. Out of habit. Out of fear that telling the truth would unravel the last threads of relationship I had with certain people. But this is *my* story. And I've learned that silence can be more violent than anything we say out loud.

So let me say it.

I. The Fetish of the Mixed Child

There's a sickness in how some white women have fetishized mixed babies—how they dream up these curated children with light eyes and caramel skin and curls just wild enough to be interesting, but tame enough to be accepted. I've seen it. I've lived it. Not just in media or the news or in someone else's essay—but in my own home, in my own body.

We don't talk enough about the harm of being raised by someone who loves your Blackness in theory but fears it in practice.

I've been asked, "What are you?" Not where are you from, not who are you—but *what* are you. As if I was chattel. As if the skin I'm in, the lineage I carry, is an experiment they're trying to decode.

I've heard white mothers describe their children by race before personality—"He's half Black and half white," they say proudly, as if the mixture itself is the whole story. As if that's the most important thing you need to know. And then they'll throw in the name—something unusual, followed by, "But we call her something easier." Not because the name's not beautiful. But because they knew what they were doing when they stamped that child with a name that screams, *I'm different. I'm Black. Expect less from me.* A name that might be beautiful in the mouth, but heavy on a job application or school roster.

Naming is sacred. It's not just a label—it's a lineage, a calling, a prayer. And yet, some white women name their children for the flavor of Blackness, but not the weight. Not the consequences. They give birth and believe love is enough—but love without awareness can still destroy. Especially when that love centers their comfort, not their child's truth.

Of course, not every white woman who has a child with a Black man did so out of fetish or fantasy. Some genuinely loved their partner. Some raised their children with intention, respect, and room for full identity. But too often, the pattern remains: children treated like trophies until they become too Black, too loud, too real.

There are white women who birth Black children and raise them to be grateful for their survival, while still policing their tone, their mess, their anger, their joy. They adore the aesthetics—but they do not make space for the rage, the sorrow, the cultural memory. They create children who are meant to be symbols—and then punish them for being whole.

They call it love, but it comes with rules. With terms. With unspoken clauses that say: "I will care for you, but you will not embarrass me."

I watch children carry names, skin, and spirit this world isn't ready for—and I refuse to let that go unnamed.

II. Flat Irony

You didn't think I'd write this whole daggon book as a Black, biracial woman and not talk about hair, did you?

From day one, my hair revealed things about me—loudly. Before I could speak, my curls told the world: she's not just white. And not just any curls—mine were thick, wavy, curly, unruly. Tangly. Snarly. Nappy. Swallowed combs, broke brushes, held sand for years. Hair that did its own thing, every day, no matter what I wanted. Growing up, I hated it.

My mom didn't know what to do with it. Not because she was white—she actually went to beauty school and was the one who taught me to cornrow—but because my hair was a whole other beast. Not just "mixed kid hair." It was wild, stubborn, full of force. It took years for me to learn how to tame it, to love it, to even *see* it as mine.

Along the way, I learned how different mixed hair care is (or should be) from Black hair care. Some things overlap, but not everything translates. The spectrum of hair textures among mixed folks is unreal. The best experiences I've had getting my hair done weren't even at Black salons—they were with Brazilians, Dominicans, or Moroccans, who knew how to respect the texture *and* the volume.

And yet, I also learned fast what hair meant in the Black community—especially when yours doesn't fit the mold. My hair was never "together." It didn't stay straight. It didn't sit down. And Black girls noticed. They were the ones most vocal about what my hair wasn't, what *I* wasn't. I hated my hair even more after that. Middle school is when I started doing hair for other mixed kids and their moms—Black, white, or in-between. I'd show them what to use, how to detangle, how to twist, how to *care*. It was more than styling. It was identity repair.

Remember when I first met my dad's side of the family, I asked one of my aunties if I could do my cousin's hair? She told me no. I was hurt, but I got it. You don't just let anybody in your hair—especially not someone who looks like me. But years later, when my granddaddy died, I showed up with Abri's hair in braids I had done myself. I was proud of that. Until someone in the family made me take them out—to show off her "good" curls instead. I'll never forget that.

Even Diamani and Abriana's dad once told me that one of the reasons he left was because I couldn't braid his hair like she could. Yeah. That was an actual excuse he gave.

Years later, Abri went to stay with my dad's family for the summer. She came back with her hair damaged. Tangled, dry, broken. I had to cut it up to her ears just to start fresh. And if *I* couldn't save it—and I've saved so many kids' heads before—then it was gone.

I had once been forbidden, and her hair was destroyed.

Now, her hair's back. Full force. Even thicker than mine ever was and all the way down to her hips. I used to think my hair was one-of-a-kind, but I've *never* seen anything like hers—not in South Africa, not anywhere. Her strands are thick, and there are *so many* of them. People say their kids have a lot of hair or their kid's hair is unique, but unless you've seen Abri, you don't know.

Hair is sacred. Hair is history. Hair is heat. And every time I've tried to flatten mine to fit, to belong, to be acceptable, something else flattened too—my joy, my pride, my self-worth.

All that flat irony.

III. The Internalized Hatred in Proximity
The closer some white people are to Blackness, the more violently they try to contain it. It's not just about biracial children. It's also about Black relatives. Black daughters. Black cousins. Black nieces. Black colleagues. Black neighbors.

There is a pattern of control masked as caretaking—where whiteness wants proximity to Blackness but only on its terms. And when that control slips, the punishment is swift: withholding affection, rewriting history, erasing names, closing doors.

They don't see it as harm. They see it as help. As grace. As saving you from yourself. And that's what makes it so hard to name—and so easy for them to deny.

Sometimes the control looks like generosity. Like, "We just want what's best for you." But the subtext is clear: *Be who we want you to be—or be nothing at all.*

I've felt this in family dynamics that don't get talked about. In spaces where whiteness insists it is "the good one" because it didn't walk away—but stayed just close enough to manage the narrative. Not close enough to understand. Not close enough to be changed.

And when you finally name what's happening, they act wounded. As if your truth is betrayal. As if your boundaries are violence.

Whiteness wants the beauty of Blackness without the burden, the rhythm without the reckoning, the bloodline without the breakdown. Because acknowledging that would mean giving up the illusion of innocence. It would mean naming the harm in the help. The control in the care. The violence in the love.

That illusion of innocence is the cornerstone of white identity. It protects the self-image of being the "good one," the helper, the ally. Letting it go would mean confronting that harm has lived in their hands—even when they meant well. And that kind of reckoning requires more than good intentions—it requires surrender.

IV. The Price of Black Compliance
At the same time, I see what happens to Black people who make themselves small to survive.
There are people who would rather keep their job than keep their voice. People who will swallow injustice, smile through disrespect, and call it professionalism. Call it growth. Call it adulting.
But I can't.

Because every time I've tried to "play the game," something in me
started to rot.
I've never been able to offer up my truth in exchange for a paycheck.
Or a seat at the table. Or a nicer version of captivity.
To me, that's backwards.
How is it that telling the truth costs us everything,
but pretending gets us promoted?
How is it that silence buys safety,
but honesty is what gets us punished?

I look at people who call me "too much,"
and I want to ask: too much for what?
Your comfort? Your denial?
Your illusion of equity?

I don't want a lifestyle that requires me to betray myself to keep it.

I remember my grandfather at the dinner table.
Quiet man. Sharp eyes. Still hands.
I must've been five or six.
I did something and he corrected me—
"We don't do that at the table."
Then something else—
"We don't do that either."
Then I tried to speak, and he stopped me again—
"We don't say that."
I sat there for a moment, confused.
And then I asked,
"Then what do we do at the table?"
And that man—stone silent most days—he laughed.
Out loud.
Because even he knew I was right to question it.

That memory lives in me.
Because I've spent years at tables

where nobody could name or explain the rules—
but everyone expected me to follow them.

And here's the truth:
Black compliance is the cost of white comfort.
And every time we choose silence for the sake of safety,
we're not just surviving—we're making a deal.
A spiritual transaction.
A modern-day corporate prostitution.

They don't need to hang us anymore.
Not when they can hire us.
Not when they can put us on payroll, dress it up in benefits,
and call our silence "professionalism."
Not when they can say:
"We want your Black brilliance,
but only if it doesn't come with Black truth."

This is not professionalism.
It's choreography.
A calculated routine that keeps us
palatable, presentable, predictable.
It is labor disguised as loyalty—
a system that survives off our self-betrayal.
A corporate contract that demands your dignity
in exchange for a direct deposit.
And the more of us who sign it, the longer the system survives.

If I'm the only one who speaks, nothing changes.
But if more of us refused—
if we stopped shrinking for the check and started standing in our
truth—they wouldn't know what to do.
Because they've built the entire system on our silence.
And they bank on us needing the job more than we need our
wholeness.

So I'll keep speaking.
Not because I have nothing to lose—
but because I'm finally willing to say it.

V. I Speak to Exist
I exist when I speak.
That's not ego. That's oxygen.
Speaking isn't performance—it's permission.
It's the only way I know I'm still alive in here.
People ask why I can't just... chill.
Why I have to say something.
Why I always notice the thing that's off,
the thing no one else wants to name.
Because I was built for it.
Because I survived off my voice
when everything else was broken.
Because my silence has never saved me—
only made me easier to use.

I speak because when I don't,
I start to vanish.
Not metaphorically—actually.
My body shrinks.
My back tightens.
My energy leaves the room before I do.

Earlier this year, my father said:
"You messed up so many good jobs.
If you woulda just kept your mouth shut..."
Yet I've always known this:
I didn't mess them up.
I just refused to disappear.
I told the truth in places that fed off my presence
but never made room for my perspective.
I named what others avoided.

Afterthought: I Can't Keep My Mouth Shut

And yes, I paid for it.
But I walked away intact. And free.
So no, I'm not keeping my mouth shut.
Not for a job.
Not for a platform.
Not for your approval.
Not to stay invited to tables I'd rather flip over.
And if that makes me difficult—so be it.
If that makes me disposable—so be it.
Because every time I speak,
I get a little bit more of myself back.
And every time I don't,
I lose ground I already fought for.

Let this be my afterthought:
I don't speak to be heard.
I speak to exist.

And I've earned the right
to never disappear again.

About the Author

Brianna Miller is a writer, mother, coach, and sacred disruptor of what was never meant to last. She was born into the in-between—Black and white, truth and silence, seen and unseen—and has spent her life daring to name what others won't.

A single mother of four, including two adopted daughters, Brianna has lived many lives in one: surviving domestic violence, rebuilding after betrayal, mothering children with disabilities, and rising as a leader in justice-centered spaces that often tried to erase her. She has been praised, punished, dismissed, and desired—all while doing the quiet, courageous work of becoming herself.

Her company, **On Paper LLC**, is both a business and a philosophy: that language creates reality, and when we name what's real, we begin to live in alignment with what matters most. Through writing, coaching, and curriculum, she helps others tell the truth about their lives and design what's next.

Brianna holds degrees and certifications in nonprofit leadership, ontological development, and executive coaching. But more than that, she holds stories—her own and those of the people she walks beside.

She is raising four brilliant children. She leads with love and fire. And she's still writing—because her story is still unfolding.

About On Paper Press

On Paper Press is a BIPOC-led publishing house rooted in liberation, healing, and narrative justice. We publish stories that rupture silence, restore dignity, and reflect the fullness of identity.

We are more than a press—we are a platform for voices long excluded. We exist to protect what power tried to erase and to print what possibility looks like. Our work centers BIPOC, queer, disabled, immigrant, and nontraditional authors with something honest to say.

Our catalog includes memoir, poetry, hybrid works, curriculum, and tools that don't just inform—they transform. We believe language is legacy, and story is strategy.

We don't just publish books. We create space for truth to live.
Learn more or submit your work at:
www.onpaperllc.com/on-paper-press

Colophon

This book was written and lived by Brianna Miller.

Designed, typeset, and published by On Paper Press
in Eden Prairie, Minnesota.

Set in Cambria font and printed using Print-on-Demand methods
through KDP/IngramSpark.

Sealed with the mark of *Authresshood* – a butterfly
born of ink and fire, *possibility and proof.*

Learn more or share your truth at:
www.onpaperllc.com